The Irish Isle

New Irish Cuisine
Traditional Irish Music

BOOKS IN THE MENUS AND MUSIC SERIES

Dinner and Dessert

Holidays

Dinners for Two

Nutcracker Sweet

Music and Food of Spain

Picnics

Dining and the Opera in Manhattan

Lighthearted Gourmet

Rock & Roll Diner

The Irish Isle

Afternoon Tea Serenade

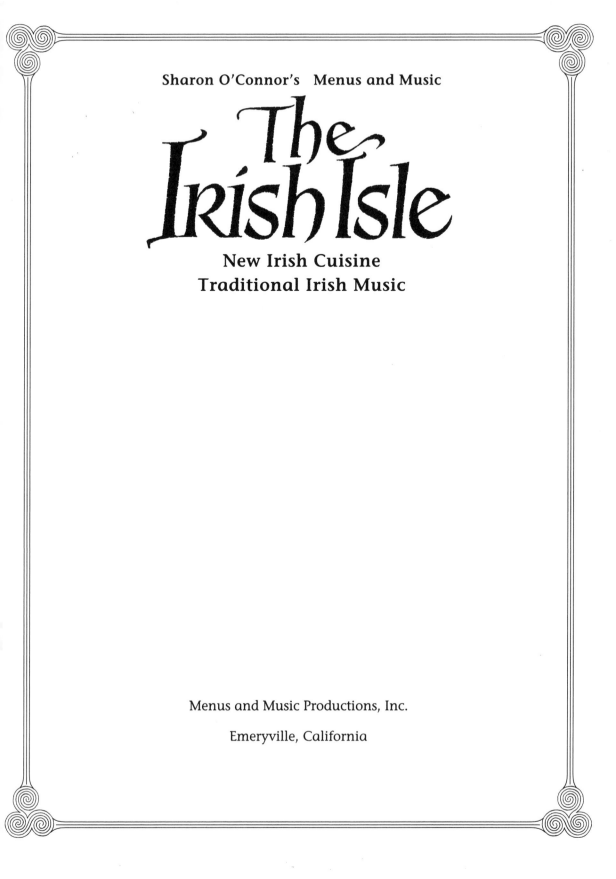

Sharon O'Connor's Menus and Music

The Irish Isle

New Irish Cuisine
Traditional Irish Music

Menus and Music Productions, Inc.

Emeryville, California

Library of Congress Catalog Card Number: 96-78371

O'Connor, Sharon

Menus and Music Volume XI

The Irish Isle

New Irish Cuisine

Traditional Irish Music

Includes Index

1. Cookery 2. Entertaining

I. Title

ISBN 1-883914-16-7 (paperback)

ISBN 1-883914-15-9 (hardcover)

Menus and Music Productions, Inc.

1462 66th Street

Emeryville, CA 94608

(510) 658-9100

Book and cover design by Michael Osborne Design, Inc.

The Drimcong House recipes on pages 87-91 are from *The Drimcong Food Affair* by Gerry Galvin, McDonald Publishing, Moycullen, County Galway, Ireland.

The Trinity College (Brian Boru) harp is reproduced by the kind permission of the Board of Trinity College, Dublin.

Cover photograph of Newport House by George Munday, The Slide File, Dublin.

Manufactured in the United States of America

10 9 8 7 6 5 4 3 2

CONTENTS

FOREWORD

Ireland must in truth be heaven, I suppose, but I must in all honesty reveal to you that Sharon O'Connor, though indeed an angel thinly disguised, did not herself in fact originate in the blessed Emerald Isle, although it is a matter of record that she has been endowed with an exalted Gaelic ancestry that encompasses a bevy of Charles O'Connors, at least one of which is reputed to have been a nobleman and an enthusiastic supporter of the legendary harper Carolan, who himself might well be the Hibernian answer to Schubert, if the question should ever arise, and she could also claim, if she so wished, a more recent relative named Molloy who composed "The Kerry Dance," and we must also recall some priceless years of familial coaching from her two cosmopolitan daughters and their very talented father, all of whom have contributed to the author's aura of charm and grace, and you'll be sure to note the omission herein of all references to shamrocks, poteen, or St. Patrick and the slithery snakes, and it's for an obvious reason, which is that I have been strenuously advised to avoid run-on sentences; go tell that to James Joyce.

As an ancient Irish-American, although of Gaelic extraction only on my mother's and father's side, I have long endured the vile canard that an Irish seven-course dinner consists of a boiled potato and a six-pack of Guinness. Hah! Now, if my dear daughter accomplishes naught else during the course of her entire career, she will have earned her father's undying applause and gratitude, for with the writing of this book she has once and for all laid that infernal duck in its grave.

In Sharon's loving portrayal, as you are soon to read, the starving land abandoned for America in the 1850s by her paternal great-grandparents is shown today to be a bountiful country that has hosted a gourmet revolution during the past fifteen years. Here, indeed, a treasury of gustatory wonders awaits at friendly castles, manor houses, and country house hotels for whoever approaches the table with knife and fork at the ready.

And when the glories of the table have overwhelmed even the most robust of appetites, as surely they will, there's always room for the most refreshing treat that Ireland has to offer. Sure and the sweetest dessert in all the world is the heavenly lilt of Irish music.

Now 'tis high time for you to share in the luck of the Irish. Gently dig in!

—Charles O'Connor

INTRODUCTION

As a child, daydreaming was a way of life for me. I grew up with the fantasy of becoming a musician and had a grandmother who fed me romantic notions about Ireland as she taught me to cook. We spent many Saturday afternoons together baking and dreaming of elegant and cozy Irish country houses nestled in acres of green meadows and ancient oaks. I'm now a grown-up professional cellist who loves cooking and fine food, and during the past two years I have had the pleasure of working on the project of my dreams.

The research for this book has led to enough sojourns in Irish castles and country manor houses to make dreams come true beyond imagination. During my visits there have been days for long walks in the countryside and hours for reading by the hearth; discussions with chefs about recipes, food, and philosophy; extraordinary dinners by candlelight; and unforgettable musical performances. I know from firsthand experience that the food in Ireland really has changed, and that traditional music is in the air everywhere, still very much alive.

During the past fifteen years or so, Ireland has experienced a culinary awakening that has won international accolades. Pioneers such as Myrtle Allen, Darina Allen, and Gerry Galvin have inspired others to create a new cuisine of remarkable quality. A new generation of chefs with great technique and fresh ideas are dedicated, generous, and passionate about what they are doing.

Many classically trained chefs are now choosing to work in Ireland because of the ready availability of superior raw products. They are creating exciting local and seasonal dishes from the wealth of fresh ingredients that this largely unpolluted land has to offer. These chefs are also guardians of Irish culinary heritage, and they include favorite traditional dishes and down-to-earth cottage staples on their sophisticated menus. Meals are served in elegant dining rooms throughout the country with friendly hospitality that's legendary. Today Ireland has a thriving food culture, and the fine dining in that country is some of the best in the world.

The contributors to this book have provided you with a connoisseur's guide to Ireland. Most of them are members of the Irish Country Houses and Restaurants Association, now simply known as *The Blue Book.* Founded in 1974, this group has established a high standard of excellence for hospitality in Ireland. This cookbook also includes menus and recipes from all ten Irish members of the prestigious Relais & Chateaux, a forty-year-old association of highly individual deluxe hotels and gourmet restaurants throughout the world. These privately owned accommodations, most in country surroundings, reflect the personality and dedication of the hotelier as well as the region in which they are located.

Destination dining in Ireland is especially romantic. First you travel on lanes meandering through some of the world's most beautiful unspoiled countryside to find yourself in an exceedingly comfortable country manor house where a welcoming fire and the warm hospitality of the resident hosts awaits. As you sit sipping a sherry in the drawing room before dinner, chatting with other house guests and choosing from the evening's menu, you have a feeling of ease probably more appropriate to the last century than to this one. Then you are escorted into a formal candlelit dining room, where you know after the first taste that you are in for a dining experience never to be forgotten. After dinner, looking out on countryside ashimmer with beauty and scarcely changed for centuries, you listen to quiet music. It seems possible to set sail for a place that is neither here nor there, and there is a moment when you sense both the way forward and the way back—the spirit is renewed.

In this cookbook, twenty-three talented chefs, each with his or her own distinctive style, provide you with a sampling of new Irish cuisine. Although the dishes reflect the food of each house and its region, the chefs chose recipes with the home cook in mind. You don't need to be a highly skilled chef to prepare any of these dishes. I have even included some of my own recipes of favorite Irish comfort foods, which I hope you'll enjoy. You can re-create an entire menu from this book or choose dishes from sev-

9

eral restaurants to make up your own menu as long as you achieve a balance of tastes. All of the contributing chefs base their cooking on top-quality fresh ingredients. The plentiful array of foods available at most markets makes it possible for you to re-create these dishes at home. The tastes, smells, and sense of warm hospitality that result from entertaining in your home are marvelous gifts that will remain long after many other memories are forgotten.

Music is a keeper of memories, and the Irish have many memories to keep. This is music felt deep in the bone. Through it we can hear ancestral voices telling us how it was, and feel the joy, ache, and pull of Ireland no matter how far away we are. In distant California, I grew up accompanying my dad's evening renditions of Irish airs and as a professional enjoyed performing arrangements of Irish music with the San Francisco String Quartet.

The beautiful music recorded here will set a mood of grace and elegance for dining, and can also be enjoyed while cooking or as an after dinner concert. Recording James Keane, Seamus Egan, Winnie Horan, and Sue Richards, four extraordinarily talented musicians, on a snowbound February weekend in New York City was an experience I will remember always. A special nod to my friend James Keane for his artistry, for his unfailing generosity, and for making sure all our paths crossed—it's been quite a journey.

In order to feel the real spirit of place that is Ireland, plan a visit and experience its pleasures for yourself. In the meantime, I hope this volume will tide you over and help you create an Irish feast in your own castle.

So here's to fine food and beautiful music together! *Bon appétit,* or rather, *bain sult as an bhia!*

—*Sharon O'Connor*

Map of Ireland

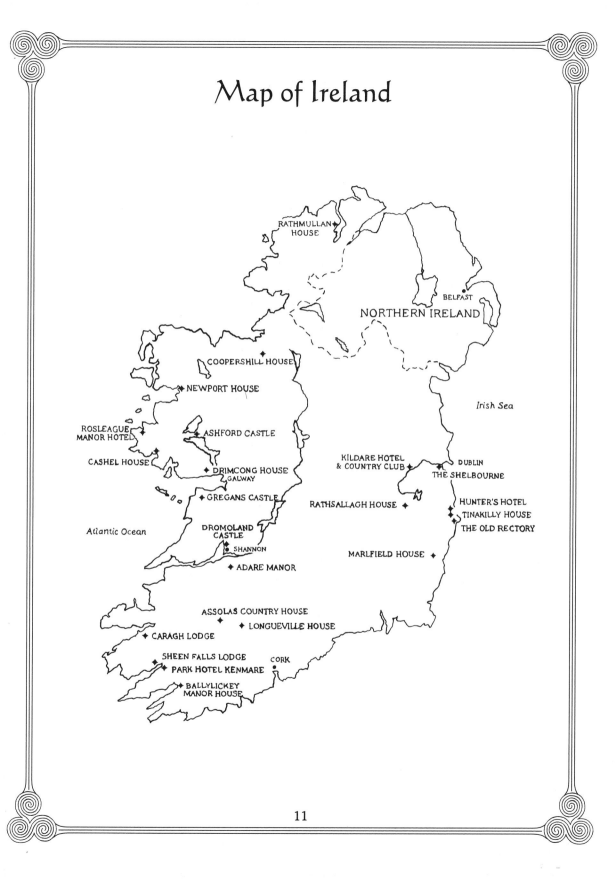

RATHMULLAN HOUSE

BELFAST

NORTHERN IRELAND

COOPERSHILL HOUSE

Irish Sea

NEWPORT HOUSE

ROSLEAGUE MANOR HOTEL

ASHFORD CASTLE

CASHEL HOUSE

DRIMCONG HOUSE
GALWAY

KILDARE HOTEL & COUNTRY CLUB

DUBLIN
THE SHELBOURNE

GREGANS CASTLE

RATHSALLAGH HOUSE

HUNTER'S HOTEL
TINAKILLY HOUSE
THE OLD RECTORY

DROMOLAND CASTLE

SHANNON

Atlantic Ocean

MARLFIELD HOUSE

ADARE MANOR

ASSOLAS COUNTRY HOUSE

LONGUEVILLE HOUSE

CARAGH LODGE

SHEEN FALLS LODGE
PARK HOTEL KENMARE

CORK

BALLYLICKEY MANOR HOUSE

MUSIC NOTES

The traditional music recorded here is performed by a quartet of virtuoso musicians. James Keane has won three consecutive Senior All-Ireland championships and is a former member of the legendary Castle Célí Band. A Dublin native and current New York resident, James is known for his astonishing technique on the button accordion and is especially esteemed for his ability to capture the spirit of Irish music. Flutist Seamus Egan is a multiple All-Ireland champion who plays eight instruments. Also a composer, his credits include the musical soundtrack for the movie *The Brothers McMullen*. Classically trained Winnie Horan is a gifted fiddler who can dash off dazzling reels and jigs and give performances of beautiful melodies that go straight to the heart. The ensemble playing and superb solo work of Celtic harp champion Sue Richards carries on a distinguished living tradition. Don Meade has graciously written the following music notes:

Many centuries of Irish tradition are reflected in this musical program. Perhaps the oldest piece on the recording is "Brian Boru's March," named for the high king of Ireland who died leading his army to victory over Viking invaders at the battle of Clontarf in 1014. Like "South Wind," it is an ancient tune from the repertoire of the harpers patronized by Ireland's noble families before English conquerors destroyed the old Gaelic order.

"Give Me Your Hand" ("Tabhair Dom Do Lamh" in the Irish language) is one of Ireland's most enduringly popular melodies. It is attributed to the harper Ruairi Dall O Cathain, whose anglicized name, Blind Rory Keane, perhaps identifies him as one of James Keane's long-lost kinsmen! James Keane and Sue Richards also play compositions by another blind harper, the great Turlough O'Carolan, whose life spanned the late seventeenth and early eighteenth centuries. "Sí Beag, Sí Mór" ("The Little Fairy Hill and the Big Fairy Hill") is reputed to be O'Carolan's first composition.

The historic Belfast harp festival of 1792, which gathered together the few remaining elderly harpers in Ireland, marked the end of the golden age of the Irish harp. The task of keeping Irish music alive was passed on to players of the uilleann pipes, fiddle, and flute. The concertina and button accordian (James Keane's favored instrument) arrived in Ireland in the mid-nineteenth century and were soon integrated into the country's musical tradition.

The lively reels and jigs on this recording, including "The Boys of Ballisodare," "Connachtman's Rambles," and the "Cup of Tea Set," are but a few of the thousands of dance tunes in the repertoire of Ireland's traditional instrumentalists. Many of these tunes are centuries old, the legacy of anonymous musicians whose compositions have long outlived their names. Some of the most beautiful and distinctive of these pieces are known as "set dances." These tunes, which include "Three Sea Captains," "The Hunt," and "Jockey to the Fair," were the musical accompaniment to virtuoso solo steps created by traveling dancing masters in the province of Munster.

"Inisheer," named for the smallest of the three rugged Aran Islands off Ireland's west coast, is a lovely melody composed comparatively recently by Thomas Walsh. The rich vocal tradition of Ireland is the source for "Carrickfergus" and "Down by the Sally Gardens," two of the most beloved of Irish airs. The words of "Carrickfergus" express the singer's longing to be in a picturesque seaside town in County Antrim. "Down by the Sally Gardens" (from *saileach*, Irish for willow) has lyrics penned by the great poet William Butler Yeats.

Down by the Salley Gardens

Down by the salley gardens my love and I did meet;
She passed the salley gardens with little snow-white feet.
She bid me take love easy, as the leaves grow on the tree;
But I, being young and foolish, with her would not agree.

In a field by the river my love and I did stand,
And on my leaning shoulder she laid her snow-white hand.
She bid me take life easy, as the grass grows on the weirs;
But I was young and foolish, and now am full of tears.

—William Butler Yeats, 1889

13

Carrickfergus

I wish I was in Carrickfergus
only for nights in Ballygrand.
I would swim over the deepest ocean
only for nights in Ballygrand.
Ah, but the sea is wide and I cannot swim over,
nor have I wings so I could fly.
I wish I could meet a handsome boatman
to ferry me over to my love and die.

My childhood days bring back sad reflections
of happy times I spent so long ago,
My boyhood friends and my own relations
have all passed on now like melting snow.

But I'll spend my days in endless roaming,
soft is the grass, my bed is free.
Ah! to be back now in Carrickfergus, on that
long road down to the sea.

And in Kilkenny it is reported there are
marble stones there as black as ink
With gold and silver I would transport her,
but I'll sing no more now till I get a drink.
I'm drunk today, and I'm seldom sober,
a handsome rover from town to town,
Ah! but I'm sick now, my days are over,
so come all ye young lads and lay me down.

Music Notes

COOK'S NOTES

Not that many years ago the idea of a book of gourmet Irish recipes would have been received with great doubts, but today Irish food is newly glamorous. In the late seventies, a gastronomic revolution began in Ireland. Chefs and restaurateurs, using the natural bounty of the land (superior produce, fish, game, beef, lamb, pork, and dairy products), have created a gourmet cooking style that draws from other European cuisines but is resolutely Ireland's own.

This culinary awakening has resulted in new takes on traditionally hearty Irish fare and regional dishes. Cooks at all levels are rediscovering their culinary heritage, based on local ingredients cooked simply and served in generous portions. What could be better than a tray of oysters washed down with some Guinness, brown bread with homemade preserves and a cup of tea, or a fillet of beef cooked to perfection along with new potatoes drizzled with sweet butter? The recipes in this book take advantage of the wealth of fresh ingredients available today and allow you to savor such festive dishes as Smoked Salmon and Goat Cheese Roulade with Champagne-Chive Dressing, Roast Rack of Lamb with Honey-Thyme Dressing, and Irish Mist Soufflé. The book also gives you an idea of where to find great food when you visit Ireland.

Irish life is intimately related to the land, with over 70 percent of the country still rural. Its coastal waters are the cleanest in Europe, the unpolluted rivers and lakes brim with fish, the woods are full of game, and the lush grazing lands are free from chemical fertilizers and pesticides. The foods that come from these unspoiled sources make possible the very best kind of cooking.

Ireland was famous for its green grass nearly two thousand years ago when a Roman geographer, Pomponius Mela, a contemporary of Christ and native of Spain, wrote his *De Situ Orbis* (Description of the World). He reported that Irish vegetation was luxurious and savory, and that if the cattle were not restrained from feeding, they would, by eating, burst!

The following is the bard Amergin's mythopoetic praise of the abundant riches of the Irish land:

I speak for Erin,
Sailed and fertile sea,
Fertile fruitful mountains,
Fruitful moist woods,
Moist overflowing lochs,
Flowing hillside springs.

The sea, mountains, woods, and lakes of Ireland are still bounteous, despite at least eight thousand years of human inhabitance. Today, Irish chefs enjoy the best natural ingredients available anywhere in Europe. Organic vegetables, free-range poultry, farm-made cheeses, and locally smoked fish remain the treasures they have always been. In the mid-1900s, many Irish embraced packaged foods, imported specialties, and fast food, and the country's fresh produce, fish, game, beef, lamb, and rich milk were ignored or not properly used. Then, during the 1980s, a new awareness of food was nurtured by a dedicated group of chefs in a few special restaurants and country house hotels. They demanded the best local vegetables, herbs, fruits, fish, lamb, and beef, and championed skilled farmers, bakers, and cheesemakers. Now in the 1990s, being a chef in Ireland is prestigious, and sons and daughters of the "best" families apply to leading Irish chefs for a chance to apprentice in their kitchens. Many chefs were trained on the continent, and although their kitchens draw much inspiration from France, they are confidently establishing their own culinary style based on fresh local ingredients.

When you visit Ireland, you will find that the new Irish cuisine is memorable for both its quality and variety. The award-winning farmhouse cheeses, sausages, lamb and beef vary from county to county, and these local specialties help travelers discover a true sense of each region. At Longueville House, the salmon is caught in the morning from the nearby Blackwater River; at Marlfield House the vegetables you admired that afternoon in the kitchen garden appear on your dinner plate; and at Assolas some of the cheeses, which rival any on earth, are made just down the road.

Cook's Notes

The cuisine of Ireland evokes both the beautiful, unspoiled countryside and the instinctive warmth and hospitality of the Irish people. Because everything is fresh, the bounty of each season is truly enjoyed: spring herbs and vegetables, summer fruits, wild salmon in season, game in winter. This makes all the difference in flavor, and it is well worth seeking out the best ingredients when you are making these recipes yourself. Look for farm-fresh organic produce, just-picked herbs, free-range chickens, high-quality cheeses, and smoked meats from your own local suppliers.

When you prepare the delicious dishes in this book, you will be participating in an updated Irish tradition that has deep roots in the past. I hope you enjoy this introduction to the new Irish cuisine!

Tinakilly House's Recipe to Beat the Seasonal Blues

You can re-create this recipe yourself, using one of the menus that follow and listening to the beautiful Irish music recorded especially for this volume.

A sip of champagne
A dash of music
A generous portion of splendid cuisine
A pinch of peace and quiet

Heat beside the flames of a roaring log fire and follow by a period of ample rest, thus allowing the finished product to reappear totally refreshed.

Adare Manor

Adare, County Limerick

Formerly home to the Earls of Dunraven, the impressive castlelike Adare Manor dates to 1720 and was extensively rebuilt in the Tudor Revival style between 1832 and 1860. The ornate great hall, reputed to be the second longest in Europe, was copied from Versailles, and the beautiful oak stairway features finely carved ravens, which are reminders of the second earl's wife, heiress to the Dunraven Castle of Wales.

In 1988, Adare Manor was transformed from a private estate into a luxurious hotel. Guests enjoy strolls through formal gardens and lush parkland on the thousand-acre estate next to the Maigue River, as well as horse riding, salmon and trout fishing, clay-pigeon shooting, and golfing on an eighteen-hole championship course designed by Robert Trent Jones. There is also a complete health and fitness center with a sauna and indoor swimming pool on the grounds.

Adare Manor's elegant public rooms include barrel-vaulted ceilings, fifteenth-century Flemish doors, crystal chandeliers, and magnificent, ornately carved wooden and marble fireplaces. Guests take afternoon tea in the drawing room, then at dinner savor the best of French and Irish cuisine in the dining rooms overlooking the garden. Afterward, they can retire to the library for a drink in front of the fireplace or join the laughter and Irish song in the Tack Room. The following dinner menu was created by chef Gerard Costelloe.

THE MENU
Adare Manor

Scallop and Vegetable Terrine with Potato-Mustard Dressing

Smoked Salmon and Goat Cheese Roulade with Champagne-Chive Dressing

Watercress and Lime Soup

Cod Tournados in Chanterelle-Chervil Broth

Caramelized Bread Pudding with Custard Sauce

Serves Six

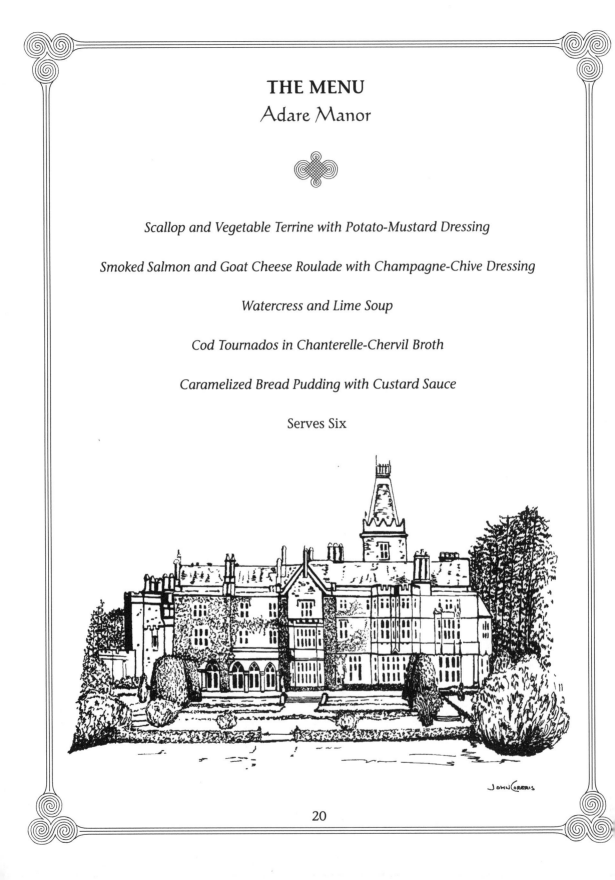

John Coreris

Scallop and Vegetable Terrine
with Potato-Mustard Dressing

Filled with a delicate scallop mousse and a variety of garden-fresh vegetables, this terrine is wrapped in thin slices of carrot.

Scallop Mousse
8 ounces (250 g) cold scallops, coarsely chopped
2 cold egg whites
Salt and ground white pepper to taste
1 cup (8 fl oz/250 ml) heavy (whipping) cream

4 ounces (125 g) julienned peeled turnip
4 ounces (125 g) julienned peeled parsnip
4 ounces (125 g) julienned peeled celery root
2 red bell peppers, seeded, deribbed, and cut into julienne
1 zucchini, cut into julienne
6 large fresh spinach leaves
4 large carrots, peeled and cut into very thin lengthwise slices

To make the scallop mousse: In a blender or food processor, purée the scallops, egg whites, salt, and pepper just until blended, about 15 seconds. Strain through a fine-meshed sieve into a medium bowl, cover, and refrigerate for 30 minutes.

In a deep bowl, whip the cream until soft peaks form. Gently fold the whipped cream into the chilled scallop mixture.

Preheat the oven to 275°F (135°C). In a large pot of salted boiling water, separately blanch the turnips, parsnips, celery root, bell peppers, and zucchini for about 2 minutes each. Drain the vegetables in a colander, pressing them with the back of a large spoon to remove all liquid. Season the vegetables with salt and pepper and pack them together, forming a cylinder. Wrap the cylinder in the spinach leaves.

Blanch the carrots in salted boiling water for 2 minutes; remove with a slotted spoon and drain on paper towels.

Line a 6-cup (48–fl oz/1.5-l) terrine mold with the carrot slices. Fill the terrine with half of the scallop mousse, place the vegetable cylinder in the center, and top with the remaining scallop mousse. Place the mold in a baking pan, fill the pan halfway up the side of the mold with water, and bake in the preheated oven for 55 minutes, or until set. Refrigerate the terrine for at least 4 hours, or until well chilled.

Just before serving, unmold the terrine by dipping it very briefly in a bowl of hot water, then inverting it on a cutting board. Thinly slice the terrine with a knife that has been dipped into hot water and arrange a slice on each of 6 plates. Serve immediately with some potato-mustard dressing.

Makes 6 servings

Potato-Mustard Dressing
6 tablespoons (3 fl oz/90 ml) olive oil
1 potato, peeled and finely chopped
2 teaspoons whole-grain mustard
2 tablespoons fresh lemon juice
Salt and freshly ground black pepper to taste
Minced fresh chives to taste

In a small sauté pan or skillet over low heat, heat the olive oil and sauté the potato until tender but not browned. Stir in the mustard and lemon juice; remove from heat and let cool. Stir in the salt, pepper, and chives.

Smoked Salmon and Goat Cheese Roulade
with Champagne-Chive Dressing

When cooking the roulade slices, use the least amount of butter possible.

Roulade

2 tablespoons clarified butter (see page 214)

4 potatoes, peeled and thinly sliced

6 ounces (185 g) St. Tolas cheese or other fresh white goat cheese

3 ounces (90 g) thinly sliced smoked salmon

Champagne-Chive Dressing

2 tablespoons champagne

6 tablespoons (3 fl oz/90 ml) olive oil

Minced fresh chives to taste

Sea salt and cracked black pepper to taste

Clarified butter for pan-frying

6 handfuls mixed baby greens

Preheat the oven to 350°F (180°C). In a medium sauté pan or skillet over medium heat, heat the clarified butter and sauté the potatoes until tender but not browned; let cool.

Arrange the potato slices on aluminum foil to form a square with the slices slightly overlapping. Roll out the cheese to the same size and cover the potato slices with the cheese. Top with a layer of smoked salmon slices. Roll up gently by tilting the aluminum foil to form a cylinder. Wrap the cylinder in the foil and refrigerate for at least 7 hours.

To make the dressing: In a small bowl, whisk together all the ingredients.

Cut the roulade into 1-inch-thick (2.5-cm) slices. Heat a large sauté pan or skillet over high heat and film with clarified butter. Quickly fry the slices until crisp on both sides.

Toss the baby greens with the dressing until lightly coated. Divide the greens among 6 plates, top with roulade slices, sprinkle with salt and pepper, and serve immediately.

Makes 6 servings

Watercress and Lime Soup

Watercress grows wild in streams all over Ireland and has been an important part of the Irish diet since ancient times. Here it is complemented by the tanginess of lime.

2 tablespoons vegetable oil
1 onion, chopped
1 leek (white part only), chopped
3 celery stalks, chopped
½ cup (3 oz/90 g) diced peeled celery root
6 cups (48 fl oz/1.5 l) vegetable stock (see page 225) or
    canned vegetable broth
2 pounds (1 kg) watercress, stemmed
1 cup (8 fl oz/250 ml) heavy (whipping) cream
Juice of 4 fresh limes
Salt and freshly ground black pepper to taste
Shavings of Parmesan cheese to taste

In a large soup pot or saucepan over medium-low heat, heat the oil and sauté the onion, leek, celery, and celery root until tender but not browned, about 7 minutes. Stir in the vegetable stock or broth and simmer for 30 minutes, stirring occasionally.

Stir in the watercress, raise the heat to high, and bring to a boil. Remove from heat, transfer to a blender or food processor, and purée.

In a deep bowl, beat the cream until soft peaks form. Gently stir the whipped cream and lime juice into the soup until well blended. Season with salt and pepper. Ladle the soup into 6 bowls, sprinkle with shavings of Parmesan cheese, and serve immediately.

Makes 6 servings

Cod Tournados in Chanterelle-Chervil Broth

1 pound (500 g) bacon strips
2 pounds (1 kg) cod or red snapper fillets

Broth
1 tablespoon butter
4 ounces (125 g) chanterelle mushrooms
½ fennel bulb, trimmed and thinly sliced
1 garlic clove, minced
1 bay leaf
⅔ cup (5 fl oz/160 ml) white port
1½ cups (12 fl oz/375 ml) fish stock (see page 217)
½ cup (4 fl oz/125 ml) heavy (whipping) cream
1 tablespoon minced fresh chervil
Clarified butter for frying

Overlap the bacon strips on a piece of aluminum foil, forming an area the same size as one layer of the fish fillets. Trim the fillets so they are equal in size, place them on top of the bacon in 1 layer, and roll the fish and bacon into a cylinder by tilting the aluminum foil. Cover the roll with the aluminum foil. Tie the roll with twine, cover with plastic wrap, and refrigerate for 2 hours.

To make the broth: Trim the chanterelle stems and mince them. In a medium saucepan, melt the butter over medium-low heat and sauté the minced chanterelle stems and the fennel for 5 minutes, or until tender. Stir in the garlic and bay leaf and sauté for another 3 minutes. Add the port, stirring to scrape up the browned bits from the bottom of the pan. Stir in the fish stock, raise the heat to high, and cook until the liquid is reduced to ½ cup (4 fl oz/125 ml). Add the chanterelles and cook for 2 minutes. Stir in the cream and chervil.

To serve, remove the plastic wrap and string from the fish roll. Cut the cod into 6 slices with the aluminum foil still on. Place a large sauté pan or skillet over medium-high heat, film the pan with clarified butter, and fry the tournados for 3 minutes on each side, or until golden brown. Ladle the broth into each of 6 shallow soup bowls. Remove the foil from the tournados, place a cod tournado in the center of each bowl, and serve immediately.

Makes 6 servings

Caramelized Bread and Butter Pudding
with Custard Sauce

An Irish childhood favorite, but even adults enjoy the wonderful contrast between the chilled custard sauce and the hot pudding.

Custard Sauce
1 cup (8 fl oz/250 ml) milk
1 vanilla bean, split lengthwise
6 egg yolks, beaten
2 tablespoons sugar

Bread Pudding
6 slices white bread, crusts removed
2 tablespoons butter at room temperature
2 cups (16 fl oz/500 ml) milk
Pinch of saffron
2 eggs, beaten
3 egg yolks, beaten
¼ cup (2 oz/60 g) granulated sugar
Almond extract to taste
Pinch of ground nutmeg
2 tablespoons raisins soaked in simple syrup (see page 224)
2 tablespoons packed brown sugar

To make the custard: Add the milk to a medium, heavy saucepan and scrape the vanilla bean pulp into it. Cut the bean into 2-inch (5-cm) pieces and add them to the milk. Bring the milk to a boil over medium heat, stirring constantly; remove from heat and set aside.

In a medium bowl, whisk the egg yolks and sugar together until thick and pale. Pour the milk mixture into the egg mixture in a slow, steady stream, whisking constantly. Stir the mixture back into the saucepan over medium heat and cook until the custard coats the back of a spoon. Refrigerate for several hours, or until ready to serve.

To make the pudding: Preheat the oven to 325°F (165°C) and butter a 4-cup (32–fl oz/1-l) baking dish. Butter the bread slices on both sides and cut them into thin slices.

In a medium, heavy saucepan, combine the milk and saffron and bring to a simmer over low heat. Stir in the eggs, egg yolks, sugar, almond extract, and nutmeg; remove from heat and set aside.

Arrange half of the bread slices on the bottom of the prepared baking dish and sprinkle with half of the raisins. Pour in half of the milk mixture and continue layering in the same order until all the bread is used. Sprinkle the top with brown sugar. Place in a baking dish and add hot water to halfway up the sides of the mold. Bake in the preheated oven for 25 minutes, or just until set.

Preheat a broiler and place the pudding about 2 inches (5 cm) from the heating element until the sugar is melted and crisp, about 30 seconds to 1 minute, being careful not to burn it.

To serve, pool the chilled custard on each of 6 plates and top with the bread pudding.

Makes 6 servings

Ashford Castle
Cong, County Mayo

Majestic Ashford Castle offers visitors lofty paneled ceilings, masterpiece paintings, antique furnishings, suits of armor, weathered battlements, and lovely views of Lough Corrib, the second largest lake in Ireland. Built in the eighteenth century from the remains of a thirteenth-century Norman castle, Ashford was the country estate of the Guinness family for almost one hundred years. Beginning in 1939, it was transformed into one of Europe's top luxury hotels.

Ashford Castle is set amid acres of formal lawns, quiet forests, and romantic gardens that are perfect for wandering. Guests enjoy salmon and trout fishing on Lough Corrib, boating, tennis on two all-weather courts, horse riding, and a nine-hole golf course on the grounds. The hotel's eighty-three spacious bedrooms and suites are decorated with beautiful fabrics and antique furnishings, and guests have a choice of two excellent restaurants, the George V with its continental and traditional menu, and the gourmet Connaught Room. After dining, they can listen to harp or piano music in the Dungeon Bar while sipping a pint or enjoying an Irish coffee.

The following menu was created by executive head chef Denis Lenihan. His acclaimed cooking features fish from Lough Corrib and the River Cong, local game and meats, organic vegetables and herbs, and Irish farmhouse cheeses. As with all the recipes in this book, you'll get the best results by using the highest quality and freshest ingredients available.

THE MENU
Ashford Castle

❧

Millefeuille of Prawns and Wild Mushrooms

Ashford's Famous Celery and Cashel Blue Cheese Soup

Roast Rack of Lamb with Honey-Thyme Dressing

Pear and Gooseberry Cake with Black Currant Compote

Serves Four

Millefeuille of Prawns and Wild Mushrooms

Two 12-by-17-inch (30-by-43-cm) filo dough sheets
6 tablespoons (3 oz/90 g) butter
6 ounces (185 g) chanterelle mushrooms
4 ounces (125 g) oyster mushrooms
20 large prawns
⅔ cup (5 fl oz/160 ml) heavy (whipping) cream
4 ounces (125 g) smoked chicken breast, cut into julienne
Salt and freshly ground black pepper to taste
1 tablespoon minced fresh parsley
3 handfuls mixed baby greens
1 cup (4 oz/125 g) sliced almonds, toasted (see page 224)

Place the 2 filo sheets on a work surface. Using a 2-inch (5-cm) round cookie cutter, cut the filo into 12 circles. In a large sauté pan or skillet, melt 2 tablespoons of the butter over medium heat and sauté the filo discs until golden brown on each side. Using a slotted spatula, transfer to paper towels to drain.

In the same pan over high heat, sauté the chanterelles and oyster mushrooms for 4 to 5 minutes; remove the mushrooms with a slotted spoon and set aside.

In the same pan over medium-low heat, sauté the prawns for 4 to 5 minutes, or until pink and opaque. Remove the prawns with a slotted spoon and set aside.

In the same pan, melt the remaining 4 tablespoons (2 oz/60 g) of the butter, whisk in the cream, and cook for 6 to 7 minutes, stirring constantly. Stir in the mushrooms, prawns, smoked chicken, salt, pepper, and parsley; remove from heat.

Ashford Castle

To serve, lay 1 filo disc in the center of each of 4 plates and top with a little filling. Place a second filo disc on top and continue making another level of layers in the same fashion. Decorate the rim of each plate with greens and sprinkle with almonds.

Makes 4 servings

Ashford's Famous Celery and Cashel Blue Cheese Soup

Cashel Blue is handmade by Jane and Louis Grubb in County Tipperary from the raw milk of their own dairy herd. If it is unavailable, substitute a soft, mild blue cheese.

2 tablespoons butter
3 celery stalks, chopped
1 onion, coarsely chopped
1 cup (4 oz/125 g) chopped leek (white part only)
4 cups (32 fl oz/1 l) chicken stock (see page 213) or canned low-salt
  chicken broth
1 pound (500 g) potatoes, peeled and diced
4 ounces (125 g) Cashel Blue cheese, crumbled (about 1 cup)
⅔ cup (5 fl oz/160 ml) heavy (whipping) cream
Salt and freshly ground black pepper to taste

In a large saucepan, melt the butter over medium heat and sauté the celery, onion, and leek for 4 to 5 minutes, or until soft but not browned. Stir in the stock or broth and bring to a boil. Add the potatoes, reduce heat to low, and simmer for 45 minutes. Remove from heat, transfer to a blender or food processor, and purée.

Return the soup to the saucepan over low heat and slowly add the blue cheese and cream, stirring constantly. Season the soup with salt and pepper. Correct the consistency of the soup, if necessary, by adding a little more cream or stock or broth. Just before serving, strain through a fine-meshed sieve. Ladle the soup into bowls and serve immediately.

Makes 4 servings

Roast Rack of Lamb with Honey-Thyme Dressing

Roasting is the most popular cooking method for lamb in Ireland, and the hazelnuts used here impart a wonderful flavor. Often served with gravy and either mint sauce or red currant jelly, here it is sweetened by a dressing of honey and thyme.

2 racks of lamb (3 chops each)
¾ cup (9 oz/280 g) honey, warmed
1 bunch fresh thyme, chopped (reserve 4 sprigs for garnish)
4 cups (16 oz/500 g) hazelnuts, toasted and peeled (see page 224)
2 tablespoons olive oil
1 cup (8 fl oz/250 ml) lamb stock (see page 217), reduced to a glaze
Salt and freshly ground black pepper to taste
½ cup (4 fl oz/125 ml) peanut oil
¾ cup (4 oz/125 g) peeled and thinly sliced celery root
2 tablespoons butter
8 baby carrots
8 baby leeks

Have your butcher remove most of the fat and the chine (backbone) from the racks. Preheat the oven to 325°F (165°C). Coat the back of the lamb racks with honey and sprinkle them with thyme. Arrange a bed of the hazelnuts in a roasting pan and place the lamb racks on top. Bake in the preheated oven for 20 to 22 minutes; remove the lamb and let it stand.

Place the roasting pan over low heat, add the reduced lamb stock, and simmer for 20 minutes. Strain the sauce (discard the hazelnuts) and season with salt and pepper.

In a medium, heavy sauté pan or skillet, heat the peanut oil over high heat until almost smoking and fry the celery root slices until golden brown. Using a slotted spoon, remove the celery root and drain on paper towels; sprinkle with salt.

Ashford Castle

In a large sauté pan or skillet, melt the butter over medium heat and sauté the carrots and leeks until just tender.

Slice the lamb racks into cutlets. Spoon a pool of the sauce into the center of 4 plates and arrange 3 lamb slices, 2 carrots, 2 leeks, and some celery root slices on top of each. Garnish each plate with a thyme sprig and serve immediately.

Makes 4 servings

Pear and Gooseberry Cake with Black Currant Compote

If you like a sweeter cake, you may want to increase the amount of sugar to offset the tartness of the gooseberries.

1¾ cups (9 oz/280 g) self-rising flour
Pinch of salt
1 teaspoon ground ginger
½ cup (4 oz/125 g) cold butter, cut into pieces
2 pears, peeled, cored, and thinly sliced
3 cups (12 oz/375 g) fresh gooseberries or raspberries
½ cup (4 oz/125 g) granulated sugar or to taste
2 eggs, beaten
½ cup (4 fl oz/125 ml) milk
Raw sugar for sprinkling
Black Currant Compote (recipe follows)

Preheat the oven to 375°F (190°C) and butter a 9-by-13-inch (23-by-32.5-cm) baking pan. In a large bowl, sift together the flour, salt, and ginger. Cut in the butter until the mixture resembles fine bread crumbs. Stir in the pears, berries, and sugar. Mix in the eggs and milk. Pour the batter into the prepared baking pan and sprinkle the top with raw sugar. Bake in the preheated oven for 25 to 30 minutes, or until the cake is golden brown and springy to the touch. Slice and serve with black currant compote.

Makes one 9-by-13-inch (23-by-32.5-cm) cake

Black Currant Compote
2 baskets (8 oz/250 g) fresh black currants or blackberries
½ cup (4 fl oz/125 ml) simple syrup (see page 224)

In a medium saucepan, combine the ingredients and simmer for 15 to 20 minutes. Serve warm.

Makes about 2 cups (16 fl oz/500 ml)

Ashford Castle

Assolas Country House
Kanturk, County Cork

Assolas Country House, a charming seventeenth-century manor house with a convivial country house atmosphere, is very much a family home. Opened to guests in 1965 by Hugh and Eleanor Bourke (founding members of the Irish Country Houses & Restaurants Association), the house is now managed with warm personal attention by Joe Bourke, with the kitchen run by Hazel Bourke, a chef of distinction.

Nine comfortably furnished bedrooms overlook either the old courtyard or the peaceful surrounding countryside. Guests enjoy strolling through the well-maintained grounds, visiting the walled kitchen garden, playing lawn tennis or croquet, or boating on the river that flows by the house and is home to a family of tame swans. (Wellingtons are available for anyone who feels like seeking out otters along the riverbank.) Assolas is a comfortable home base for taking day trips to the Dingle Peninsula and the Ring of Kerry, salmon fishing on the famous Blackwater River, riding at nearby stables, or playing golf on one of the many courses in southwestern Ireland.

At the end of the day, guests return to the welcome of a log and peat fire in the drawing room, where aperitifs are served before dinner. A superb meal awaits in the candlelit dining room. Hazel Bourke offers choices from a seasonal menu, a daily menu, or a combination of the two. Her exceptional cooking emphasizes the natural fresh flavors of superior ingredients without overelaboration, and she gracefully updates and refines traditional foods with the imaginative use of organic regional produce, fresh seafood, Irish cheeses, and meats from her own butcher. A trolley of irresistible desserts and excellent farmhouse cheeses completes the meal. The following holiday dinner-party menu was created by Hazel Bourke for Menus and Music.

THE MENU
Assolas Country House
Festive-Season Dinner Party

Smoked Salmon Mousse and Filo with Cooleeny Cheese and Cranberry Sauce

Sautéed Prawns with Béarnaise Sauce

Garden Salad with Herb Vinaigrette

Spiced Beef

Braised Red Cabbage

Dauphinoise Potatoes

Passion Fruit Parfait with Red Fruit Compote

Serves Eight

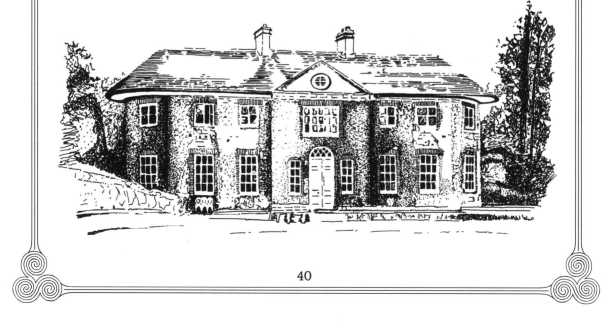

Smoked Salmon Mousse

This delicious appetizer may be made up to 2 days before serving.

7 ounces (220 g) smoked salmon, chopped
Squeeze of fresh lemon juice
½ cup (4 fl oz/125 ml) half-and-half
¼ cup (2 fl oz/60 ml) heavy (whipping) cream, lightly whipped
Melba toast or rye bread for serving

In a blender or food processor, blend the smoked salmon and lemon juice for 2 minutes. With the machine on low speed, gradually pour in the half-and-half; do not over beat. Transfer to a bowl and gently fold in the whipped cream, cover with plastic wrap, and refrigerate for 4 hours, or until ready to serve.

Just before serving, pipe the salmon mousse onto melba toast or rye bread.

Makes 8 appetizer servings

Filo with Cooleeny Cheese and Cranberry Sauce

This quick and easy appetizer melts in the mouth. The flavor of Cooleeny falls somewhere between a Camembert and Brie cheese.

Eight 12-by-17-inch (30-by-43-cm) sheets filo dough
½ cup (4 oz/125 g) unsalted butter, melted
8 ounces (250 g) Cooleeny or Brie cheese
3 tablespoons fresh cranberry sauce

Preheat the oven to 400°F (200°C) and lightly grease a baking sheet. Stack the filo and cover it with a towel.

On a work surface, arrange 1 filo sheet with a long side facing you and brush lightly with some butter. Top with a second filo sheet and brush lightly with butter. Cut the stacked filo crosswise into 4 equal strips. Place a cube of the cheese near one corner of each strip and top with ½ teaspoon of the cranberry sauce. Fold the corner of filo over to enclose the filling and form a triangle. Continue folding the strip, maintaining the triangle shape. Place, seamside down, on the prepared baking sheet. Repeat to make a total of 16 triangles. Bake in the preheated oven for 10 minutes, or until the filo is golden brown. Serve warm.

Makes 16 pieces, or 8 appetizer servings

Assolas Country House

Sautéed Prawns with Béarnaise Sauce

Allow 5 prawns per person as a starter portion.

Béarnaise Sauce
3 tablespoons white wine vinegar
6 peppercorns, crushed
½ bay leaf
Pinch of ground mace
1 tablespoon minced shallot
2 egg yolks
6 tablespoons (3 oz/90 g) unsalted butter, cut
    into tablespoon-sized pieces
1 tablespoon minced fresh tarragon
1 tablespoon minced fresh parsley
1 tablespoon minced fresh chives
Salt and freshly ground black pepper to taste

2 tablespoons butter
40 medium prawns, shelled and deveined
Salt and freshly ground pepper to taste
8 lemon wedges for garnish
Fennel fronds for garnish

To make the béarnaise sauce: In a small saucepan over medium heat, combine the vinegar, peppercorns, bay leaf, mace, and shallot and boil until the liquid reduces to 1 tablespoon; remove from heat, strain through a fine-meshed sieve (discard spices), and set aside.

In the top of a double boiler over barely simmering water, whisk together the egg yolks and vinegar mixture. Gradually whisk in the butter, 1 tablespoon at a time. Continue whisking until the sauce has thickened. Stir in the tarragon, parsley, chives, salt, and pepper. Keep the béarnaise sauce warm over tepid water until ready to serve.

Assolas Country House

In a large sauté pan or skillet, melt the butter over medium heat and sauté the prawns for 3 to 4 minutes, or until evenly pink and opaque. Season with salt and pepper. Divide among 8 warm salad plates, top with béarnaise sauce, and garnish with lemon wedges and fennel.

Makes 8 first-course servings

Garden Salad with Herb Vinaigrette

Herb Vinaigrette
1 tablespoon Dijon mustard
Salt and freshly ground black pepper to taste
1 tablespoon minced shallot
1 garlic clove, crushed
½ cup (4 fl oz/125 ml) white wine vinegar
1 cup (8 fl oz/250 ml) olive oil

8 handfuls mixed baby greens with fresh herbs such as chervil, basil, flat-leaf parsley, and burnet, and edible flowers such as nasturtium and borage

To make the vinaigrette: In a blender or food processor, blend the mustard, salt, pepper, shallots, garlic, and vinegar. With the machine running, gradually pour in the olive oil and blend until emulsified.

Just before serving, toss the fresh greens with the herb vinaigrette until lightly coated.

Makes 8 servings

Spiced Beef

Spiced beef is a traditional Christmas dish in Ireland and makes an excellent alternative to turkey. It is delicious served cold as well as warm and is best sliced very thinly. Be sure to allow about 10 days for its preparation.

4 pounds (2 kg) boned top or bottom round beef
1 teaspoon saltpeter*
1 cup (8 oz/250 g) salt
½ cup (3½ oz/105 g) packed brown sugar
4 cups (32 fl oz/1 l) water, or more as needed
1 tablespoon ground black pepper
1 tablespoon crushed juniper berries
2 teaspoons ground ginger
1 teaspoon ground nutmeg
1 teaspoon minced fresh thyme
2 teaspoons ground mace
3 teaspoons ground allspice
3 teaspoons ground cloves
2 bay leaves, crushed

In a large pot or Dutch oven, combine the beef, saltpeter or curing salt, and brown sugar and add enough water to cover the meat. Bring to a boil over medium heat and boil for 10 minutes, then remove from heat and let cool slowly. Place the beef and liquid in a large glass or earthenware bowl, cover, and refrigerate for 1 week, turning the beef each day.

In a small bowl, stir together the pepper, juniper berries, ginger, nutmeg, thyme, mace, allspice, cloves, and bay leaves until well blended. Drain the beef and rub it with the spice mixture. Return the beef to the refrigerator for 3 to 4 days; turn and rub the beef with the spices daily.

The day of serving, place the beef and enough water to cover in a large pot over medium heat. Bring to a boil, skimming off any foam that rises to the surface. Reduce the heat to medium low and simmer for 2½ to 3 hours, or until the beef is very tender. Remove from heat and allow the beef to

Assolas Country House

cool in its liquid. To serve, slice thinly or, for cold beef, refrigerate until chilled and then slice thinly. Spiced beef will keep for at least 1 week and it also freezes well.

Makes 8 servings

Saltpeter, or curing salt, is available from butchers.

Braised Red Cabbage

In addition to beef, this dish goes well with game and pork.

6 tablespoons (3 oz/90 g) butter
3 pounds (1.5 kg) red cabbage, shredded
2 large tart apples, peeled, cored, and sliced
1 onion, chopped
3 tablespoons sugar
3 tablespoons white wine vinegar
Salt and freshly ground black pepper to taste

In a large sauté pan or skillet over medium heat, melt the butter and sauté the cabbage for 5 minutes. Using a slotted spoon, transfer the cabbage to a bowl. In the same pan, sauté the apples and onion until the onion is translucent, about 7 minutes. Raise heat to medium high and stir in the cabbage, sugar, and vinegar. Bring to a boil, cover, reduce heat to low, and cook for 10 minutes, or until tender. Season with salt and pepper. Serve warm.

Makes 8 servings

Dauphinoise Potatoes

This dish of scalloped potatoes is delicious and easy to make.

3 pounds (1.5 kg) potatoes, peeled and thinly sliced (6 to 7 cups)
4 cups (32 fl oz/1 l) milk
1 fresh thyme sprig
1 tablespoon butter
Salt and freshly ground black pepper to taste
Grated fresh nutmeg
1 cup (4 oz/125 g) grated white cheddar or Gruyère cheese
½ cup (4 fl oz/125 ml) heavy (whipping) cream

Preheat the oven to 375°F (190°C) and lightly butter an 8-cup (64–fl oz/2-l) baking dish 1½ to 2 inches (4 to 5 cm) deep.

In a large saucepan, combine the potatoes, milk, thyme, butter, salt, pepper, and nutmeg and bring to a boil over medium heat. Reduce heat to low and simmer for about 10 minutes, or until the potatoes are tender.

Using a slotted spoon, remove the potatoes and transfer half of them to the prepared baking dish. Sprinkle over half the cheese, half the cream, and salt and pepper. Top with the remaining potatoes and sprinkle with the remaining cheese and cream.

Bake in the preheated oven for 45 minutes to 1 hour, or until crisp and golden on top.

Makes 8 servings

Passion Fruit Parfait with Red Fruit Compote

Although passion fruit is, of course, not native to Ireland, such tropical fruits are imported and used for fresh desserts.

¼ cup (2 fl oz/60 ml) water
¾ cup (6 oz/185 g) sugar
3 egg whites
1 tablespoon fresh lemon juice
10 passion fruits, peeled, seeded, and puréed
1 cup (8 fl oz/250 ml) heavy (whipping) cream, lightly whipped
Red Fruit Compote (recipe follows)
Fresh lemon balm or mint sprigs for garnish

Line a 9-by-5-inch (23-by-13-cm) loaf pan with plastic wrap. In a small saucepan, combine the water and sugar, bring to a boil over medium heat, and cook until the syrup reaches a temperature of 250°F (120°C).

In a large bowl, beat the egg whites until foamy. Whisk in the lemon juice and continue beating until soft peaks form. Turn the mixer to low speed and beat in the hot syrup in a thin stream until stiff, glossy peaks form. Allow the meringue to cool. Gently fold the passion fruit purée and cream into the meringue. Turn into the prepared loaf pan, cover, and freeze.

To serve, allow the parfait to soften slightly at room temperature, then slice with a knife that has been dipped in hot water. Serve with red fruit compote and garnish with lemon balm or mint.

Makes 8 servings

Red Fruit Compote

This compote can be made with a variety of fruits, depending on what is ripe. Alter the amount of sugar used in the syrup depending on the sweetness or acidity of the fruit.

Syrup

½ cup (4 oz/125 g) vanilla sugar (see page 224)
1 cup (8 fl oz/250 ml) water

4 cups (1 lb/500 g) loganberries, raspberries, black and/or red currants, gooseberries, halved strawberries, and/or rhubarb, cut into 1-inch (2.5-cm) pieces

To make the syrup: In a small saucepan, combine the sugar and water and stir over low heat until the sugar dissolves. Bring the syrup to a boil, reduce heat, and simmer for 2 minutes.

Add the rhubarb pieces, if using, to the syrup and poach until they are tender but still retain their shape. Using a slotted spoon, remove the rhubarb and place in a glass serving bowl. Poach loganberries, gooseberries, and currants separately in the same way.

Add the strawberries and raspberries, if using, to the fruits in the serving bowl. (They do not need to be poached, as the heat of the syrup is enough.) Pour the hot syrup over and let cool.

Makes about 5 cups (2 ½ lb/1.25 kg)

Ballylickey Manor House
Bantry Bay, County Cork

Home of the Franco-Irish Graves family for four generations and currently owned and managed by Christiane and George Graves, Ballylickey Manor House is nestled in beautiful gardens with sweeping views of Bantry Bay. Built about three hundred years ago as a hunting lodge for Lord Kenmare, the house was remodeled in 1950, partially destroyed by fire in 1984, and is now restored to its original appearance.

Truly a family affair, the manor contains mementos of George's uncle, the poet Robert Graves; refined interior decoration by Christiane; and award-winning flower gardens and grounds designed by George's mother, Kitty Graves. Guests enjoy sitting before a log fire in the elegant drawing room, with its seventeenth-century furniture and fine collection of paintings, and stay either in comfortable bedroom suites in the manor house itself or in one of the attractive chalets that surround the heated outdoor swimming pool. A member of Relais & Chateaux, Ballylickey also offers private trout and salmon fishing and is an ideal center from which to tour the beautiful southwest of Ireland.

Meals at Ballylickey are served in the formal candlelit dining room in the main house, and in the summer months a restaurant and adjoining sitting-room bar are set up by the swimming pool. The following recipes were created by George Graves.

THE MENU
Ballylickey Manor House

Tomato and Thyme Tartlets

Veal Sauté

Irish Cassis

Serves Two

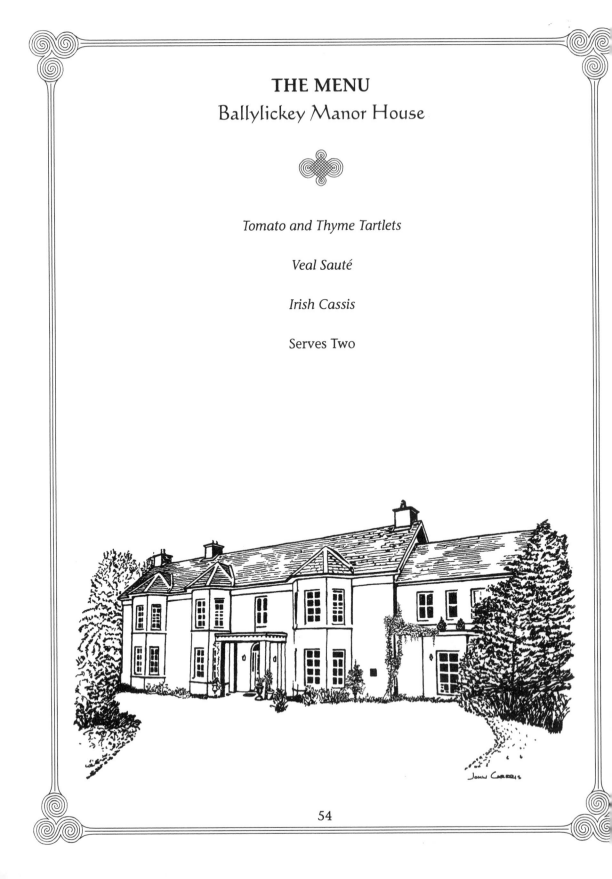

Tomato and Thyme Tartlets

12 large fresh spinach leaves
2 tomatoes, peeled, seeded, and diced (see page 220)
Salt and freshly ground black pepper to taste
2 fresh thyme sprigs

Preheat the oven to 425°F (220°C). Lightly oil two 5-inch-diameter (13-cm) molds. In a pot of boiling water, blanch the spinach leaves for 1 minute. Using a slotted spoon, transfer to paper towels to drain, carefully spreading the leaves out.

Line the prepared molds with the spinach leaves, leaving part of each leaf outside the rim.

Divide the tomato between the 2 molds, season with salt and pepper, and top with a thyme sprig. Fold the spinach leaves over to cover the filling and bake in the preheated oven for 15 minutes.

Makes 2 servings

Veal Sauté

It is best to begin this dish the day before serving, so the flavors will have time to marry.

2 tablespoons butter
1 pound (500 g) veal, cubed
2 onions, chopped
4 small carrots, diced
1 celery stalk, diced
1 fresh thyme sprig
1 bay leaf
1 garlic clove, minced
1 cup (8 fl oz/250 ml) dry white wine
1 cup (8 fl oz/250 ml) chicken stock (see page 213) or
   veal stock (see page 225)
1 handful linden (lime blossom) leaves, optional
¼ cup (2 fl oz/60 ml) heavy (whipping) cream
Chopped fresh chives and linden (lime blossom) leaves for garnish

In a large sauté pan or skillet, melt the butter over medium heat and sauté the veal until lightly browned on all sides. Using a slotted spoon, transfer to a plate. Add the onions, carrots, celery, thyme, bay leaf, and garlic and sauté until the onions are translucent, about 7 minutes. Add the veal, wine, stock, and optional linden leaves and simmer for 20 minutes.

Using a slotted spoon, remove the veal and set aside on a plate. Over high heat, bring the sauce to a boil and reduce it by half. Stir in the veal and remove from heat. Let cool and refrigerate overnight. Return the pan to medium heat, heat through and stir in the cream. Divide between 2 plates and garnish with chives and linden leaves.

Makes 2 servings

Irish Cassis

This simple dessert deserves the ripest and most delicious fruit.

4 cups (1 lb/500 g) fresh red currants, black currants, strawberries,
   and/or raspberries
¾ cup (6 fl oz/180 ml) water
⅔ cup (5 oz/155 g) sugar
1 envelope plain gelatin
½ cup (4 fl oz/125 ml) heavy (whipping) cream
1 cup custard sauce, chilled (see page 215)

Divide 2½ cups (10 oz/315 g) of the currants or berries evenly between 2 large wineglasses.

In a blender or food processor, purée the remaining 1½ cups (6 oz/185 g) fruit. Strain through a fine-meshed sieve.

Pour ¼ cup (2 fl oz/60 ml) water in a cup and sprinkle the gelatin over. Let sit for 5 minutes. In a small saucepan, combine the sugar and remaining ½ cup (4 fl oz/120 ml) water and bring to a boil over medium heat. Stir in the fruit purée and gelatin mixture. Pour over the fruit in the glasses and refrigerate until chilled.

In a deep bowl, beat the cream until soft peaks form. Fold into the custard sauce and serve with the cassis.

Makes 2 servings

Caragh Lodge
Caragh Lake, County Kerry

A mid-Victorian villa overlooking beautiful Caragh Lake and the Macgillycuddy Reeks, Ireland's highest mountains, Caragh was originally built as a fishing lodge. In addition to marvelous salmon and trout fishing, today's guests enjoy boating, swimming, golfing, and horse riding. The Ring of Kerry is less than a mile away, and the sandy beaches of Dingle Bay are within a ten-minute drive. Comfortable furnishings and welcoming log fires make the lounges of the main house a perfect place to end the day.

Proprietors Mary and Graham Gaunt went to County Kerry in 1985 intending to buy a little summer house; they came across Caragh Lodge, which was for sale, and to their own surprise ended up buying it and running a small luxury hotel. Set in an enchanting, award-winning garden with azaleas, camelias, rhododendrons, lilacs, magnolias, and rare subtropical shrubs, Caragh Lodge has retained its original country house character, complete with cornice moldings, marble fireplaces, antique furnishings, and old prints. Fifteen restful and delightfully decorated rooms open out onto the grounds.

Mary Gaunt created the following delicious recipes, which reflect the dining room's emphasis on local seafood, salmon from Caragh Lake, succulent Kerry lamb, garden-grown vegetables, home-baked breads, and tempting desserts.

THE MENU
Caragh Lodge

Seafood Sausages with Chive Sauce

Cream of Parsnip Soup

Noisettes of Lamb with Sorrel-Mint Cream Sauce

Queen of Puddings with Plum Sauce

Serves Four

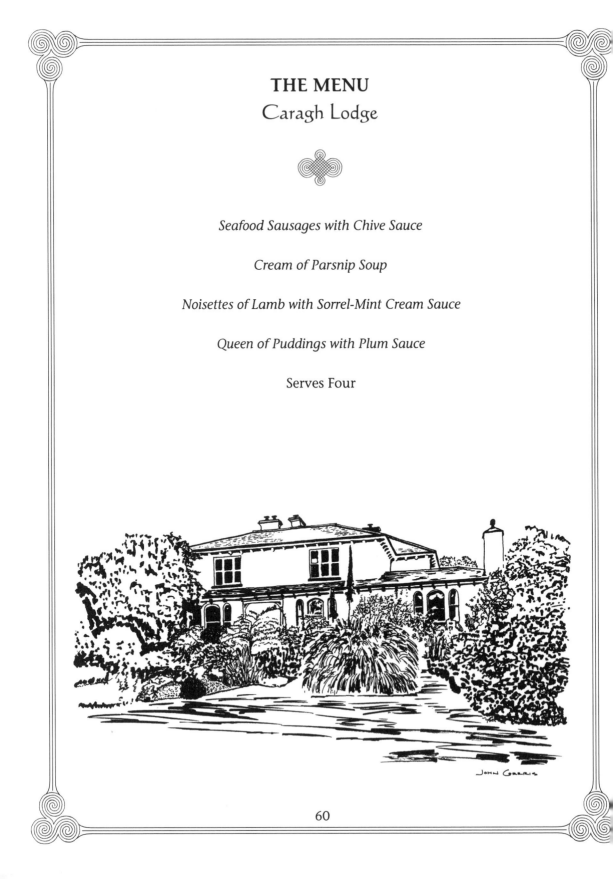

Seafood Sausages with Chive Sauce

12 ounces (375 g) salmon
1 tablespoon unsalted butter
4 ounces (125 g) brill or monkfish, finely diced
4 ounces (125 g) scallops, finely diced
¼ teaspoon salt
¼ teaspoon ground black pepper
2 teaspoons minced fresh chives
1 egg white
½ cup (4 fl oz/125 ml) heavy (whipping) cream
1 cup (2 oz/60 g) fine fresh bread crumbs
2 tablespoons butter

Chive Sauce
3 tablespoons dry white wine
3 tablespoons white wine vinegar
1 tablespoon minced shallots
Pinch of ground white pepper
1 tablespoon heavy (whipping) cream
¾ cup (6 oz/185 g) unsalted butter, cut into small pieces
1 tablespoon minced fresh chives

Finely dice 4 ounces (125 g) of the salmon. In a large sauté pan or skillet, melt the unsalted butter over medium heat and sauté the brill or monkfish, diced salmon, and scallops for 5 minutes, or until opaque. Remove from heat and season with salt, pepper, and chives; set aside.

In a blender or food processor, purée the remaining 8 ounces (250 g) salmon. Add the egg white, salt, and pepper and process until smooth. Place the puréed fish mixture in a bowl set in a bowl of ice and gradually whisk in the cream. Add the fish. Cool and refrigerate for 30 to 40 minutes.

Put 1 large tablespoon of sausage mixture onto a piece of plastic wrap and shape into a sausage. Tie a knot at each end. Repeat with the rest of the mixture.

Bring a large pot of water to a simmer and poach the sausages for 7 minutes. Drain and let cool. Remove the plastic wrap and roll the sausages in the bread crumbs. In a large sauté pan or skillet, melt the butter over medium heat and fry the sausages until golden.

To make the sauce: In a small saucepan, combine the wine, vinegar, shallots, and pepper and bring to a boil over high heat; boil until the liquid reduces to about ½ tablespoon. Add the cream and boil again until the cream begins to thicken. Beat in the butter a few pieces at a time, keeping the sauce just warm enough to absorb the butter. Add the chives and serve immediately with the seafood sausages.

Makes 4 servings

Cream of Parsnip Soup

Soup has been a staple in the Irish diet for centuries and is served today at almost every main meal, both winter and summer.

2 tablespoons butter
1 large onion, finely chopped
3 parsnips, scrubbed and diced
1 potato, peeled and diced
2 cups (16 fl oz/500 ml) chicken stock (see page 213)
  or canned low-salt chicken broth
½ teaspoon curry powder
Salt and freshly ground black pepper to taste
Heavy (whipping) cream for topping (optional)

In a large sauté pan or skillet, melt the butter over medium heat and sauté the onion for 5 minutes, or until translucent; do not let the onion brown. Stir in the parsnips and potatoes. Pour in the chicken stock or broth and bring to a boil. Reduce the heat to low and simmer for about 20 minutes, or until the vegetables are tender.

Remove from heat and transfer to a blender or food processor and purée. Return to a clean pan over medium heat. Stir in the curry powder, salt, and pepper and cook for another 8 minutes. Ladle into shallow soup bowls and serve with a swirl of cream if desired.

Makes 4 servings

Noisettes of Lamb with Sorrel-Mint Cream Sauce

The use of sorrel in Irish cooking goes back to pre-Christian times, and several varieties of mint grow all over Ireland. This sorrel-mint cream sauce complements the flavor of lamb superbly.

1 large loin of lamb, boned and trimmed of fat
Salt and freshly ground black pepper to taste
1 tablespoon olive oil
1 fresh rosemary sprig

Sorrel-Mint Cream Sauce
⅓ cup (3 fl oz/80 ml) dry white wine
1 tablespoon dry vermouth
1 shallot, minced
1 cup (8 fl oz/250 ml) chicken stock (see page 213)
   or canned low-salt chicken broth
⅞ cup (7 fl oz/220 ml) heavy (whipping) cream
6 fresh sorrel leaves, minced
6 fresh mint leaves, minced

Fresh mint sprigs for garnish

Preheat the oven to 425°F (220°C). Season the lamb with salt and pepper. In a Dutch oven or large heavy pot over medium heat, heat the olive oil and brown the lamb on all sides. Place a rosemary sprig on top of the lamb and bake in the preheated oven for about 8 minutes. Remove from the oven and let sit for 5 minutes.

To make the sauce: Place the pot over medium-high heat and add the white wine, vermouth, and shallot; bring to a boil and reduce by half. Add the stock or broth and reduce to ¼ cup (2 fl oz/60 ml). Pour in the cream, reduce heat to low, and simmer for 5 minutes. Add the sorrel and mint and cook for 1 minute.

Caragh Lodge

To serve, slice the lamb and arrange on 4 plates. Pour the warm sauce around and garnish with mint sprigs.

Makes 4 servings

Queen of Puddings with Plum Sauce

Tart, slightly underripe plums will be mellowed by the wine and sugar in this sauce.

1½ cups (3 oz/90 g) fresh white bread crumbs
2 cups (16 fl oz/500 ml) milk
2 tablespoons butter
Grated zest of 1 lemon and 1 orange
3 eggs, separated
2 tablespoons plus 1 cup (8 oz/250 g) sugar
½ cup (5 oz/155 g) raspberry jam, warmed

Plum Sauce
12 ounces (375 g) plums, halved and pitted
⅓ cup (3 oz/90 g) sugar
½ cup (4 fl oz/125 ml) dry white wine

Preheat the oven to 325°F (165°C). Butter a 4-cup (32–fl oz/1-l) oven-proof casserole dish or 6 individual ramekins. Place the bread crumbs in a medium bowl.

In a medium saucepan, combine the milk, butter, and zests and bring to a simmer over medium-low heat.

In a large bowl, whisk the egg yolks and 2 tablespoons of the sugar together. Gradually whisk in the milk mixture until blended. Strain the custard through a fine-meshed sieve into the bowl of bread crumbs and let sit for 15 minutes. Spoon the mixture into the casserole or ramekins. Bake in the preheated oven for 25 minutes, or until lightly set. Remove from the oven and spread the top with the jam.

Preheat the oven to 350°F (180°C). In a large bowl, beat the egg whites until soft peaks form. Add half of the 1 cup (8 oz/250 g) sugar and beat until the whites are thick and glossy. Gently fold in the remaining sugar. Pile the meringue on top of the pudding and bake in the preheated oven for about 10 to 15 minutes, or until the meringue is lightly browned.

Caragh Lodge

To make the plum sauce: In a medium saucepan over medium-low heat, combine all ingredients and simmer until the plums are soft. With the back of a wooden spoon, press the plums through a fine-meshed sieve. Serve the sauce with the pudding.

Makes 6 servings

Cashel House
Cashel, County Galway

Cashel House Hotel stands at the head of Cashel Bay and is tucked away in a forty-acre estate of flowering shrubs and woodland paths. Opened as a hotel in 1968, it has since gained an international reputation for comfort and excellent food in a quiet, relaxing atmosphere. (In 1969, General and Mme. DeGaulle spent two weeks of their Irish holiday here.) Warm and welcoming, perfect for long, relaxing stays, Cashel House received the Gilbeys Award for the highest standard of Irish hotelmanship in 1990; won the Best Irish Garden award in 1983 and 1987; and is a member of Relais & Chateaux.

Dermot and Kay McEvilly manage the hotel with friendly personal attention, and their Irish wolfhound, Ri (Irish for "King"), greets guests with enthusiasm. Comfortable sofas, fireplaces, and fresh flowers are found throughout the house, and each of the seventeen charming bedrooms are furnished with antiques. Cashel House has its own tennis court, private beach, rowboats, and riding trails, and golfing and ocean fishing are close by.

The dining room menu features superbly prepared fruits and vegetables grown in Cashel House's organic gardens; Connemara lamb; Irish cheeses; and lobsters, mussels, clams, scallops, and salmon straight from Cashel Bay. A carefully chosen international wine list complements the menu. The following recipes were created by Dermot McEvilly.

THE MENU
Cashel House

Smoked Salmon Pâté

Lobster Bisque

Scallops in White Wine Sauce

Turbot with Mustard Cream Sauce

Carrageen Mousse with Rum Sauce

Serves Four

JOHN CORERIS

Smoked Salmon Pâté

This pâté makes a delicious appetizer and is also wonderful picnic fare.

4 ounces (125 g) smoked salmon, chopped
Juice of ½ fresh lemon
1 tablespoon chopped onion
4 ounces (125 g) cream cheese at room temperature
2 hard-cooked eggs
2 tablespoons heavy (whipping) cream
Salt and freshly ground black pepper to taste

    In a blender or food processor, purée the smoked salmon until smooth. Add the lemon juice, onion, and cream cheese and process until smooth. Add the remaining ingredients and blend for 15 seconds. Scrape into a 2-cup (16–fl oz/500-ml) ramekin and refrigerate at least 30 minutes, or until ready to serve.

Makes about 1½ cups (12 oz/375 g)

Lobster Bisque

A perfectly elegant way to begin a special-occasion dinner. This bisque is best made 1 or 2 days before serving.

1 lobster, female if possible*
3 cups (24 fl oz/750 ml) lobster stock (see page 218),
   chicken stock (see page 213), or canned low-salt chicken broth
½ cup (4 oz/125 g) unsalted butter
½ cup (2½ oz/75 g) all-purpose flour
3 cups (24 fl oz/750 ml) half-and-half or light cream
Salt and freshly ground pepper to taste

Bring a large stockpot of salted water to a furious boil. Kill the lobster by making an incision in the back of the shell where the chest and tail meet. Cut the lobster in half horizontally, keeping the shell halves intact. Reserve the lobster coral. Plunge the lobster into the boiling water, return to a boil, and cook for 8 minutes. Remove the lobster from the pot and plunge it into a bowl of ice water to stop the cooking process. Shell the lobster and remove the meat; reserve the shell to make stock, if you like. Slice some of the tail meat and reserve it for the garnish.

In a blender or food processor, combine the lobster claw meat with a little of the stock and purée; strain through a fine-meshed sieve into a bowl. Add the lobster coral to the blender or food processor and purée.

In a large, heavy saucepan, melt the butter over medium-low heat, stir in the flour, and stir for 2 minutes; do not let the mixture brown. Stir in the stock and simmer for 15 minutes. Remove from heat and slowly stir in the cream, salt, and pepper. Let cool, then cover and refrigerate.

Return the soup to the saucepan and cook the bisque over medium-low heat for 2 to 3 minutes; do not allow it to simmer.

Ladle the lobster bisque into 4 shallow soup bowls, garnish with diced lobster meat, and serve immediately.

Makes 4 servings

The female lobster contains red roe, or coral, that will turn the bisque a beautiful coral pink.

Scallops in White Wine Sauce

Scallops are readily found off the coast of Ireland and are much enjoyed for their subtle flavor and texture.

1 cup (8 oz/250 g) mashed potatoes for decoration
1½ cups (12 fl oz/375 ml) dry white wine
1½ cups (12 fl oz/375 ml) fish stock (see page 217)
2 tablespoons minced shallots
3 cups (24 fl oz/750 ml) heavy (whipping) cream
¾ cup (6 oz/185 g) butter, cut into pieces
Salt and freshly ground black pepper to taste
Fresh lemon juice to taste
1 pound (500 g) sea scallops, quartered

Put the mashed potatoes in a pastry bag and pipe the potatoes around the edges of 4 scallop shells.

In a medium saucepan, bring the wine, stock, and shallots to a boil over high heat and cook to reduce the liquid by half. Stir in the cream and cook until the sauce is thick enough to lightly coat the back of a spoon. Add the butter one piece at a time, beating well after each addition. Season with salt, pepper, and lemon juice. Fold in the scallops and simmer for 2 minutes, or until the scallops are opaque.

Preheat the broiler. Spoon the scallops and sauce into the decorated scallop shells and arrange the shells on a baking sheet. Place the scallop shells 4 inches (10 cm) from the heating element and broil until lightly browned, 1 or 2 minutes.

Makes 4 servings

Cashel House

Turbot with Mustard Cream Sauce

Turbot holds together well when poached in this way. You may substitute halibut, sea bass, or sole.

4 turbot fillets
Salt and freshly ground black pepper to taste
1 shallot, minced
1 cup (8 fl oz/250 ml) dry white wine
½ cup (4 fl oz/125 ml) fish stock (see page 217)
1¾ cups (14 fl oz/440 ml) half-and-half
2 tablespoons heavy (whipping) cream, whipped
1½ tablespoons butter
1 teaspoon Dijon mustard
½ cup (4 oz/125 g) butter
Salt and freshly ground black pepper to taste
Fresh lemon juice to taste

Preheat the oven to 400°F (200°C). Butter a shallow baking dish. Season the fillets with salt and pepper and place them in the prepared baking dish. Sprinkle the shallot over. Add the wine and stock, cover with aluminum foil, and bake in the preheated oven for 15 minutes, or until the fish begins to flake. Remove the fish from the oven and keep warm.

In a medium saucepan over high heat, bring the stock to a boil and cook to reduce the liquid by half. Stir in the half and half and cook until the sauce thickens enough to coat the back of a spoon. Add the butter in small amounts, beating after each addition. Stir in the mustard. Remove from heat and fold in the whipped cream. Season with salt, pepper, and lemon juice.

Preheat the broiler. Arrange 1 fillet on each of 4 heatproof plates and cover the fish with sauce. Lightly brown under the preheated broiler and serve immediately.

Makes 4 servings

Cashel House

Carrageen Mousse with Rum Sauce

Carrageen is a bland-tasting seaweed found along the Irish shoreline. A rich source of agar jelly, it is used in Ireland for thickening sweet and savory dishes instead of gelatin and is available from natural foods stores.

4 ounces (125 g) dried carrageen, rinsed
2 cups (16 fl oz/500 ml) milk
1 cup (8 fl oz/250 ml) heavy (whipping) cream
¼ cup (2 oz/60 g) sugar
2 tablespoons rum
Squeeze of fresh lemon juice
2 egg whites
Rum Sauce (recipe follows)

In a medium saucepan, combine the carrageen and the milk and slowly bring to a boil over medium-low heat. Reduce heat to low and simmer for 10 to 15 minutes, or until the carrageen exudes jelly. Strain through a fine-meshed sieve.

In a deep bowl, whip the cream until stiff peaks form. Gently fold the whipped cream into the carrageen mixture. Stir in the sugar, rum, and lemon juice until well combined.

In a large bowl, whisk the egg whites until stiff, glossy peaks form. Gently fold the egg whites into the mousse. Pour the mousse into 4 individual ramekins or large wine glasses and refrigerate for at least 2 hours, or until ready to serve. Serve with rum sauce.

Makes 4 servings

Cashel House

Rum Sauce

1 cup (8 fl oz/250 ml) heavy (whipping) cream
2 tablespoons sugar
2 tablespoons rum

In a deep bowl, whip the cream until soft peaks form. Beat in the sugar and rum.

Makes about 2 cups (16 fl oz/500 ml)

Coopershill House

Riverstown, County Sligo

Dating back to 1774, Coopershill is a fine Georgian mansion that combines the spaciousness and elegance of earlier times with the utmost in modern comfort. Home to seven generations of the O'Hara family from the time it was built, the house is currently managed by Lindy and Brian O'Hara.

Coopershill guests enjoy a world of tranquility in an idyllic setting. The mansion stands in the center of a five-hundred-acre estate of farm and woodlands that provides many opportunities for hiking, boating, fishing, and wildlife watching. Guests also enjoy nearby beaches, a championship golf course, and the spectacular mountains and lakes of Yeats country. The hotel's six spacious guest bedrooms have original four-poster or canopy beds and heirloom furnishings.

In the elegant dining room, candlelit dinners, a choice of excellent wines, and gracious service combine to create an inviting atmosphere. During cooler evenings, the room is warmed by cheerful turf fires, and guests partake of a hearty Irish meal cooked by Lindy O'Hara. Imagine eating the following dishes under ancient family portraits and sparkling candelabra, then enjoying a warming nightcap before retiring to your regal Georgian bedroom.

THE MENU
Coopershill House

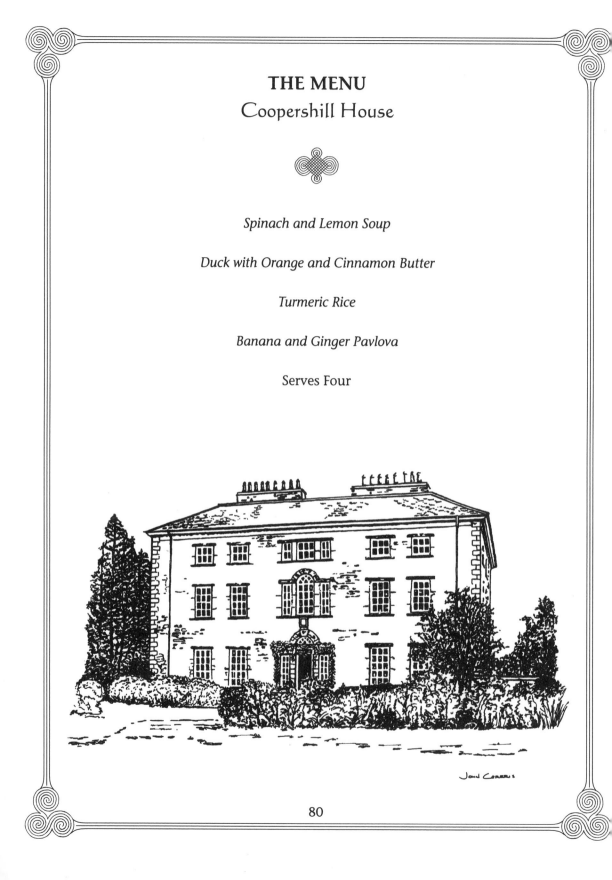

Spinach and Lemon Soup

Duck with Orange and Cinnamon Butter

Turmeric Rice

Banana and Ginger Pavlova

Serves Four

Spinach and Lemon Soup

This soup is particularly good when made with young, tender spinach.

4 tablespoons (2 oz/60 g) butter
2 onions, chopped
2 pounds (1 kg) fresh spinach, stemmed, or three 10-ounce (315-g)
  packages frozen spinach, thawed
Grated zest and juice of 1 lemon
4 cups (32 fl oz/1 l) chicken stock (see page 213) or canned low-salt
  chicken broth
Salt and freshly ground black pepper to taste
4 tablespoons (2 fl oz/60 ml) half-and-half or plain yogurt

In a large saucepan, melt the butter over medium-low heat and sauté the onion until translucent, about 7 minutes. Add the spinach, lemon zest and juice, stock or broth, salt, and pepper. Bring just to the boil, reduce heat to low, and simmer for 30 minutes. Remove from heat, let cool, and transfer to a blender or food processor; purée. Return the soup to a clean saucepan over medium heat and heat through. Ladle the soup into 4 shallow soup bowls and top each with 1 tablespoon half-and-half or yogurt.

Makes 4 servings

Coopershill House

Duck with Orange and Cinnamon Butter

Serve this dish with the following recipe for turmeric rice and fresh peas or green beans.

4 boneless duck breast halves, skin on
4 tablespoons (2 oz/60 g) butter, cut into small pieces
Finely grated zest and juice of 2 oranges
1 teaspoon ground cinnamon
1 teaspoon sugar
Salt and freshly ground black pepper to taste
1 teaspoon arrowroot
1 tablespoon water

Preheat the oven to 375°F (190°C). Place the duck breasts in a baking pan, skin-side up. Prick the skin all over with a sharp skewer and dot the surface with butter.

In a small bowl, mix the orange zest and juice together and pour this over the duck. In another small bowl, mix the cinnamon, sugar, salt, and pepper together and sprinkle the mixture over the duck. Bake the duck in the preheated oven for about 1 hour, basting once.

Remove from the oven and transfer the duck breasts to a hot platter. Skim off as much fat as possible from the baking pan, leaving behind the juice and browned bits from the duck. In a small bowl, blend the arrowroot with the water; stir this mixture into the liquid in the baking pan. There should be about ½ cup (4 fl oz/125 ml) liquid. Place the baking pan over high heat and bring the sauce to a boil. Remove from heat and strain through a fine-meshed sieve into a hot sauceboat.

Makes 4 servings

Coopershill House

Turmeric Rice

1 cup (7 oz/220 g) long-grain white rice
2 tablespoons butter
1 onion, thinly sliced
1 teaspoon ground turmeric
Salt and freshly ground black pepper to taste

Wash the rice in a strainer under cold running water. In a medium saucepan over medium heat, combine the rice and enough cold water to cover the rice by 1 inch (2.5 cm). Simmer without stirring for 15 minutes, or until the rice is almost tender. Remove from heat and strain; run a little boiling water throught the rice to separate the grains.

In a large sauté pan or skillet, melt the butter over low heat and sauté the onion until translucent. Stir in the turmeric, salt, and pepper and cook for 5 minutes, or until the onion is tender. Add the rice and cook until hot, taste and adjust the seasoning, and serve immediately.

Makes 4 servings

Banana and Ginger Pavlova

4 egg whites
1 cup (8 oz/250 g) sugar
Pinch of cream of tartar
1 cup (8 fl oz/250 ml) heavy (whipping) cream
4 ounces (125 g) crystallized ginger in syrup, drained
   (reserve the syrup) and chopped finely (about ½ cup)
2 bananas, sliced

Preheat the oven to 350°F (180°C). Butter an 8-inch (20-cm) flan pan with a removable bottom and line the bottom with parchment or waxed paper.

In a large bowl, beat the egg whites until soft peaks form. Gradually beat in the sugar and cream of tartar until stiff, glossy peaks form. Spoon this mixture evenly into the prepared pan. Make a round depression in the center and, using the tip of a skewer, make little swirls in the meringue all around the edge, lifting the skewer up sharply each time to leave a tiny peak. Place the pan in the preheated oven for 5 minutes. Lower the heat to 250°F (120°C) and bake for 1 to 2 hours, or until the meringue is light, dry, and crisp. Let cool, then wrap in airtight plastic wrap until needed.

In a deep bowl, whip the cream until stiff peaks form. Add the chopped ginger and a little of the reserved syrup. Stir in the sliced bananas. Just before serving, spoon the ginger-banana-cream into the center of the meringue.

Makes 4 servings

Drimcong House
Moycullen, County Galway

Drimcong House is an extraordinary restaurant set in Gerry and Marie Galvin's lovely seventeenth-century home. The personable owners are among the most acclaimed of Ireland's restaurateurs. In 1990 and 1991, Drimcong received the Supreme Award of Excellence for Restaurants from the Irish tourist board; it has won successive Egon Ronay stars; and it was praised by Taste Magazine as "a beacon of inspiration in Ireland."

Gerry Galvin was one of the chefs who started the cooking revolution in Ireland and has been called the chef laureate of new Irish cuisine. He has an elegant touch with natural foods and a rare talent to let "ingredients taste of themselves," as he puts it. McKenna's Bridgestone Guide describes his cooking as "very generous in spirit, motivated by a hungry creativity, and . . . distinctly Irish." The following recipes have been chosen from Galvin's own cookbook, *The Drimcong Food Affair*.

Lovingly restored Drimcong House is a wonderful setting for the sixty-seat restaurant. Turf fires in crisp weather and polished oak tables are backdrops for delicious Irish dishes, beautifully presented. The menu changes weekly and features organic fruits and vegetables from Marie's garden, fish from the lake just outside, Connemara lamb, and seafood from Galway Bay. Gerry and his talented kitchen staff also offer a selection of vegetarian dishes and a children's menu. Galvin thinks children should be taught to eat, just as they are taught to read and play music—after all, they are the restaurant customers of the next generation!

Galvin is an active member of the Irish branch of Euro-Tocques, the European Community organization of cooks formed in 1986 to enable chefs to take a lead in demanding the highest standards in food production and in using and promoting local foods. The Irish branch, one of the most active in Europe, supports quality products and encourages and protects the small producers who are the backbone of excellent food production.

THE MENU
Drimcong House

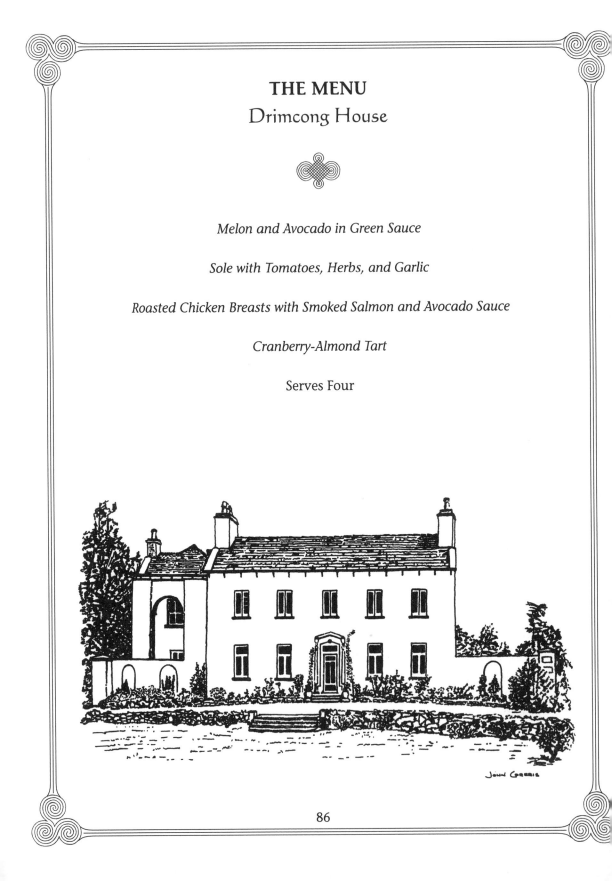

Melon and Avocado in Green Sauce

Sole with Tomatoes, Herbs, and Garlic

Roasted Chicken Breasts with Smoked Salmon and Avocado Sauce

Cranberry-Almond Tart

Serves Four

Melon and Avocado in Green Sauce

A beautifully light and refreshing summer salad.

Green Sauce
Juice of 3 lemons
Juice of 2 oranges
Half an avocado, peeled, pitted, and chopped
2 cups (3 oz/90 g) mixed fresh herbs such as mint, lemon balm,
    parsley, chervil, fennel, chives
2 teaspoons honey
Salt and freshly ground black pepper to taste

1 honeydew melon, peeled, seeded, and quartered
1 ripe avocado, peeled, pitted, and quartered

    To make the green sauce: In a blender or food processor, combine all
the ingredients and purée.

    Cut the melon and avocado quarters into fans. Arrange the fans of
melon and avocado on each of 4 plates, pour some green sauce over, and
serve immediately.

Makes 4 servings

Sole with Tomatoes, Herbs, and Garlic

Serve this delicious dish with risotto or boiled potatoes.

2 tablespoons olive oil

4 green onions, including some of the green, chopped

6 tomatoes, peeled, seeded, and chopped (see page 220)

3 garlic cloves, crushed

1 teaspoon anchovy paste

1 teaspoon pesto (see page 220)

1 tablespoon chopped mixed fresh herbs such as chives, parsley,
   sorrel, and fennel fronds

Juice of ½ lemon

Salt and freshly ground black pepper to taste

Four 6-ounce (185-g) sole fillets

Preheat the broiler. In a small sauté pan or skillet over medium heat, heat the olive oil and sauté the green onions until tender, about 3 minutes. Add the tomatoes and garlic and sauté for 1 minute. Stir in the anchovy paste, pesto, lemon juice, herbs, salt, and pepper; remove from heat.

Spread the tomato mixture evenly over the sole fillets and broil under the preheated broiler for 5 minutes, or until the fish is opaque throughout. Serve immediately.

Makes 4 servings

Roasted Chicken Breasts with Smoked Salmon and Avocado Sauce

4 boneless chicken breast halves, skin on
Salt and freshly ground black pepper to taste
4 slices smoked salmon
¼ cup (2 fl oz/60 ml) sunflower oil

Avocado Sauce
¼ cup (2 fl oz/60 ml) dry white wine
½ cup (4 fl oz/125 ml) chicken stock (see page 213) or
  canned low-salt chicken broth
1 cup (8 fl oz/250 ml) heavy (whipping) cream
Juice of ½ lemon
1½ ripe avocados, peeled, pitted, and chopped
Salt and ground white pepper

Preheat the oven to 450°F (230°C). Season the chicken breasts with salt and pepper. Make an incision along half the length of the narrow side of each breast to form a cavity and insert a smoked salmon slice in each breast.

In a large ovenproof sauté pan or skillet over medium-high heat, heat the oil and fry the chicken breasts for 1 minute on each side. Bake the chicken in the preheated oven for 15 minutes, turning once.

While the chicken is baking, make the avocado sauce: In a medium saucepan, combine the wine and stock or broth, bring to a boil, and cook to reduce the liquid to 1 tablespoon; remove from heat.

In a blender or food processor, purée the reduced wine mixture, cream, lemon juice, avocados, salt, and pepper.

When the chicken is cooked, remove the skin and pat each breast dry. Arrange a chicken breast on each of 4 plates, pour the avocado sauce over, and serve immediately.

Makes 4 servings

Cranberry-Almond Tart

Drimcong House includes this delicious tart on their pre-Christmas menus, and it is always in demand at their annual food sale, held the Sunday before Christmas.

Pastry
1 cup (5 oz/155 g) unbleached all-purpose flour
¼ cup (2 oz/60 g) sugar
Pinch of salt
5 tablespoons (2½ oz/75 g) cold butter
1 egg, lightly beaten
½ teaspoon vanilla extract

Filling
¾ cup (6 oz/185 g) butter at room temperature
¾ cup (6 oz/185 g) sugar
2 eggs, lightly beaten
1 cup (5½ oz/170 g) blanched almonds, ground
2 drops almond extract
1 cup (4 oz/125 g) fresh cranberries
¼ cup (1 oz/30 g) sliced almonds

To make the pastry: In a large bowl, combine the flour, sugar, and salt. Cut in the butter with a pastry blender or 2 knives until the mixture is crumbly. Using a fork, quickly stir in the egg and vanilla to form a soft dough. Cover and refrigerate for 2 hours before rolling out.

To make the filling: In a medium bowl, cream the butter and sugar together until light and fluffy. Add the eggs one at a time, beating to blend thoroughly. Stir in the ground almonds and almond extract until well blended.

Preheat the oven to 375°F (190°C). On a lightly floured surface, roll out the pastry dough into a 13-inch-diameter (32.5-cm) circle. Line a 12-inch (30-cm) tart pan with the pastry, trim the edges, prick the pastry all over with a fork, and line it with a square of aluminum foil. Fill the foil with dried beans or pie weights and bake the pastry in the preheated oven for 10 minutes, or until light golden. Remove from the oven, remove the foil with the beans or weights, and fill the tart shell with the almond filling. Spread the cranberries on top and sprinkle with sliced almonds. Bake in the preheated oven for 45 to 50 minutes, or until the tart is set in the middle.

Makes one 12-inch (30-cm) tart; serves 10

Dromoland Castle
Newmarket-on-Fergus, County Clare

Situated on a 350-acre estate of beautiful parkland and forests, this magnificent castle was once the ancestral seat of the O'Briens, direct descendants of Brian Boroimhe (Boru), high king of Ireland in the tenth century. Dromoland itself dates back to the sixteenth century, although the present main building was not completed until 1826. It was transformed into a luxurious resort hotel in 1963, and reminders of the castle's historic past are everywhere: in the wood and stone carvings, magnificent paneling, original oil paintings, and romantic walled gardens.

Guests at Dromoland enjoy a stay in "old Ireland" while experiencing modern luxury. Recreational activities include golf, croquet, biking, tennis, fishing, horse riding, and boating, as well as visiting Bunratty Castle and Folk Park, King John's Castle, Craggaunowen Castle, and the nearby Cliffs of Moher. The hotel's romantic bedrooms and suites have beautiful views and are sumptuously decorated with antique furnishings, custom-designed draperies and carpets, and fresh flowers.

Dromoland's elegant restaurant is considered one of the best in Ireland, and its crystal chandeliers, crisp linens, flickering candles, and views across Lough Dromoland provide a perfect setting for fine food. The menu features superbly prepared fresh produce, seafood, lamb, and beef, complemented by an outstanding selection of wines from the cellar. Guests can enjoy a pre-dinner cocktail in the Library Bar and, after dinner, join in singing Irish songs. Executive chef Jean-Baptiste Molinari created the following dinner menu.

THE MENU
Dromoland Castle

Panfried Kinvara Oak-smoked Salmon with Horseradish Cream

Ballynacally Duck in Guinness and Honey

Brown Bread Soufflé

Serves Four

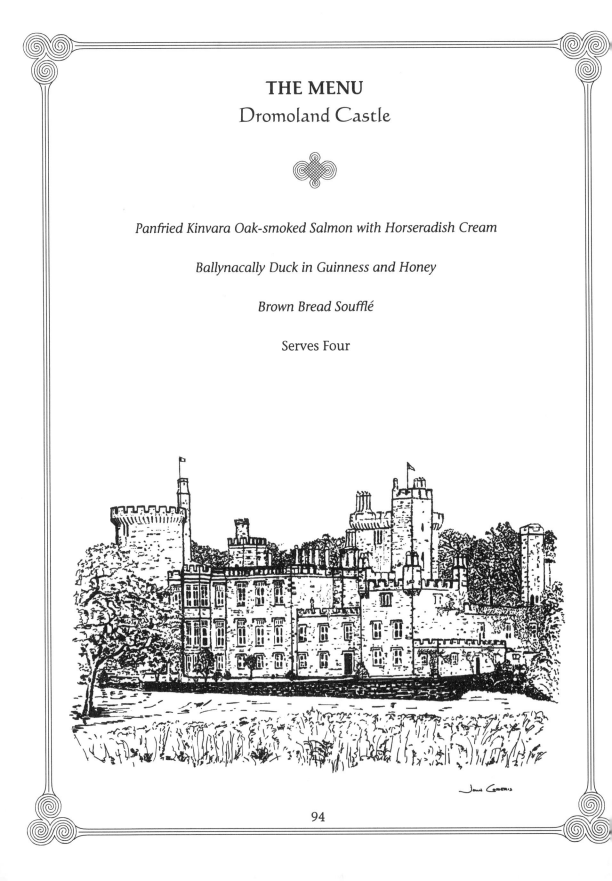

Panfried Kinvara Oak-smoked Salmon
with Horseradish Cream

Oak-smoked wild salmon is highly esteemed in Ireland and is one of the country's best-known specialty foods. Serve this perfect starter with Guinness or white wine.

12 slices Kinvara or other oak-smoked salmon
Freshly ground black pepper to taste
Olive oil for panfrying
¼ cup (2 fl oz/60 ml) whipped cream
Grated fresh horseradish to taste, or 2 tablespoons
   prepared horseradish
8 fresh chervil or parsley sprigs
4 teaspoons diced seeded tomato (see page 220)
Minced mixed fresh herbs such as chives, parsley, and dill for garnish

   Trim each slice of smoked salmon to 3 to 4 inches (7.5 to 10 cm) in length and 1 to 2 inches (2.5 to 5 cm) in width and season with pepper. Place a large sauté pan or skillet over high heat, film the pan with olive oil, and fry the salmon slices for 10 to 15 seconds on one side only.

   Arrange 3 salmon slices, fried-side up, on each of 4 plates. In a small bowl, combine the whipped cream and horseradish. Spoon or pipe the horseradish cream onto the plates. Place 2 chervil or parsley springs and 1 teaspoon tomato on each plate and sprinkle with some of the minced herbs.

Makes 4 servings

Ballynacally Duck in Guinness and Honey

1 duck, Ballynacally preferred, about 5 pounds (2.5 kg), trussed
Vegetable oil for brushing
2 tablespoons honey, or more to taste
1 tablespoon packed brown sugar
1 cup (8 fl oz/250 ml) Guinness stout
Pinch *each* ground nutmeg and cinnamon
8 to 10 whole cloves
1 cup (8 fl oz/250 ml) chicken stock or duck stock (see pages 213
 or 216), or canned low-salt chicken broth
Pinch *each* salt and freshly ground black pepper

Preheat the oven to 475°F (245°C). Place the duck in a roasting pan, brush with vegetable oil, pierce the duck all over with a fork, and bake in the preheated oven for 10 to 12 minutes, or until browned.

In a medium, heavy saucepan over low heat, combine the honey, brown sugar, Guinness, ground spices, and cloves and simmer for 10 minutes. Stir in the stock or broth and continue cooking for 15 minutes. Strain through a fine-meshed sieve and season with salt and pepper to taste.

Reduce the oven heat to 300°F (150°C). Spoon the fat out of the roasting pan. Cover the duck with the sauce and bake for 60 to 75 minutes, basting occasionally. Bake until the juices run clear when pierced with a fork. If the sauce tastes too bitter at the end of the cooking time, add a little more honey. Remove from the oven and let sit for a few minutes before carving.

Makes 4 servings

Dromoland Castle

Brown Bread Soufflé

Caramelized bread crumbs give this soufflé its rich flavor and crunchy texture.

1 cup (8 fl oz/250 ml) milk
½ vanilla bean, split lengthwise
2 egg yolks
¼ cup (2 oz/60 g) granulated sugar
3 tablespoons all-purpose flour
2 cups (4 oz/125 g) fresh brown bread crumbs (see page 157)
½ cup (3½ oz/105 g) plus 2 tablespoons packed brown sugar
4 egg whites
1 tablespoon sugar
½ tablespoon fresh lemon juice
Whiskey-flavored custard sauce (see page 215)

Butter a 6-cup (48–fl oz/1.5-l) soufflé dish and sprinkle it with sugar. In a medium, heavy saucepan, combine the milk and vanilla bean and bring just to the boil over medium heat, stirring constantly; remove from heat. Whisk the egg yolks, sugar, and flour together until pale in color. Gradually whisk the hot milk mixture into the egg yolk mixture. Pour the mixture back into the saucepan and bring to a boil over medium heat, stirring constantly. Remove from heat and let cool. Remove the vanilla bean.

Preheat the oven to 375°F (190°C). Spread the bread crumbs on a baking sheet and sprinkle them with the brown sugar. Bake in the preheated oven until browned and crunchy.

In a large bowl, whisk the egg whites until soft peaks form. Beat in the sugar and lemon juice and continue beating until stiff, glossy peaks form. Stir the bread crumbs into the pastry cream. Stir in one-fourth of the egg whites until well blended. Gently fold in the remaining egg whites. Spoon into the prepared soufflé dish and bake in the preheated oven for 10 minutes, or until puffed and lightly browned. Serve immediately with the custard sauce.

Makes 4 servings

Dromoland Castle

Gregans Castle

Ballyvaughan, County Clare

Standing alone at the foot of Corkscrew Hill near the Burren, Gregans Castle was originally the home of the Martyn family, who built it in the late eighteenth century to replace their home in the old castle nearby. The comfortable country house is now an elegant small hotel owned and managed by Peter, Moira, and Simon Haden. The Hadens' additions to the house have been made in sympathy with the old building, and it is now an oasis that provides seriously luxurious accommodation and warm hospitality.

Gregans Castle offers unforgettable views of the Burren, a spectacular area of gray limestone moonscape with rare Arctic, Alpine, and Mediterranean wildflowers and tombs and dolmens built five thousand years ago. The entire region contains unexpected wealth for both the botanist and the explorer of prehistoric ruins. The beautiful gardens surrounding Gregans Castle boast an unusually large variety of plants, including some rare subtropical shrubs from the gardens of Cashel House. Inside the hotel, all bedrooms are exquisitely furnished and decorated in the country house style, and blazing turf fires, friendly smiles, and an obliging staff ensure guests' comfort.

Sumptuous offerings in the dining room feature creatively prepared local foods, especially Burren lamb and seafood from nearby Galway Bay, and a carefully selected wine list complements the menu. A nightly performance of beautiful harp music makes the meal even more enjoyable. Before dinner, guests congregate for aperitifs in the charming Corkscrew Room, where lunch is served during the day. After dinner, they take coffee or tea beside a turf fire in the library with its antique books and Raymond Piper's paintings of unusual Burren flora. At Gregans Castle, the following menu is followed by petits fours and coffee.

THE MENU
Gregans Castle

Asparagus, Quail Egg, and Chervil Tartlets

Pheasant and Duck Consommé

Steamed John Dory on Leek and Spinach Cakes with Cucumber-Dill Sauce

Chocolate Soufflé

Serves Four

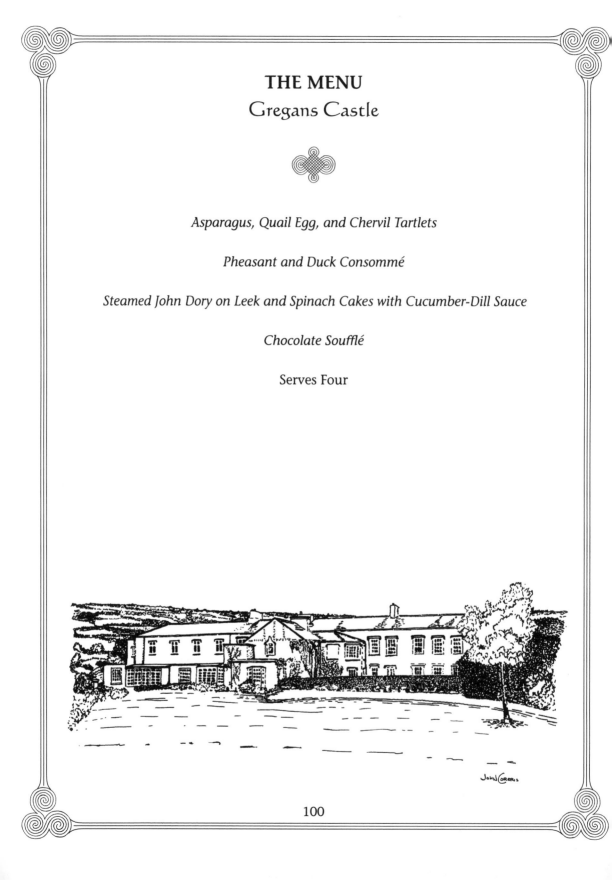

Asparagus, Quail Egg, and Chervil Tartlets

1 recipe pastry dough, chilled (see page 219)
1 egg
3 egg yolks
1 cup (8 fl oz/250 ml) heavy (whipping) cream
⅔ cup (5 fl oz/160 ml) milk
Pinch *each* salt and ground nutmeg
2 tablespoons minced fresh chervil
6 quail eggs, hard cooked
1 cup (4 oz/125 g) asparagus tips, blanched

Preheat the oven to 375°F (190°C). On a lightly floured board, roll the pastry dough out to a thickness of ⅛ inch (3 mm). Cut out four 6-inch (15-cm) circles. Line four 5-inch-diameter (13-cm) tart shells with the pastry and trim the edges. Prick the bottom of the pastry with a fork. Line the shells with aluminum foil and fill with dried beans or pie weights. Bake in the preheated oven for 8 minutes. Remove the foil and weights and bake until the pastry is golden brown, 10 to 13 minutes. Let cool.

In a medium bowl, whisk the egg, egg yolks, cream, milk, salt, and nutmeg until well blended. Stir in the chervil. Slice the quail eggs in half lengthwise and place them in the tartlet shells with the asparagus. Fill each shell almost to the top with the egg mixture. Place the shells on a baking sheet and bake in the preheated oven for 20 minutes, or until set.

Makes 4 tartlets

Pheasant and Duck Consommé

8 ounces (250 g) uncooked pheasant and duck leg meat, minced
2 egg whites
Salt to taste
4 cups (32 fl oz/1 l) pheasant stock (see page 221) or
  reduced chicken stock or broth (see page 213)
1 cup (4 oz/125 g) finely chopped mixed vegetables (onion, celery,
  leek, carrot)
Bouquet garni: 3 fresh parsley sprigs, 2 fresh thyme sprigs, and
  1 bay leaf tied in a cheesecloth bag
3 whole black peppercorns
4 ounces (125 g) *each* pheasant and duck breast meat
Salt and freshly ground pepper to taste
1 tablespoon clarified butter (see page 214)

In a large, heavy saucepan, combine the leg meat, egg whites, salt, and 1 cup (8 fl oz/250 ml) of the stock. Add the finely chopped vegetables, the remaining 3 cups (24 fl oz/750 ml) stock, the bouquet garni, and the peppercorns. Bring slowly to a boil, stirring frequently. Boil rapidly for 5 to 10 minutes, reduce heat to low, and simmer gently for 1½ to 2 hours without stirring. Strain through a double layer of cheesecloth. Remove all fat. Season with salt and pepper.

Season the pheasant and duck breast meat with salt and pepper. In a medium sauté pan or skillet over medium heat, melt the butter, add the pheasant and duck meat to the pan, and cook until browned on both sides. Slice the breast meat and divide it among 4 shallow soup bowls. Ladle hot consommé into each bowl and serve at once.

Makes 4 servings

Steamed John Dory on Leek and Spinach Cakes with Cucumber-Dill Sauce

John Dory, also known as St. Peter's fish, is a lean fish with a delicate flavor. Flounder or sole fillets may be substituted in this dish.

Leek and Spinach Cakes
1 tablespoon butter
1½ cups (6 oz/185 g) diced leek (white part only)
1 bunch fresh spinach, stemmed, blanched, and chopped
Salt and freshly ground black pepper to taste

Four 6-ounce (185-g) John Dory, flounder, or sole fillets, skinned
1 cup (8 fl oz/250 ml) fish stock (see page 217)
⅔ cup (5 fl oz/160 ml) dry white wine
1 cup (8 fl oz/250 ml) heavy (whipping) cream
⅔ cup (3½ oz/105 g) diced seeded cucumber, blanched
1 tablespoon minced fresh dill
Salt and ground white pepper to taste
Minced fresh chives, chervil, or parsley for garnish

To make the cakes: In a large sauté pan or skillet, melt the butter over medium heat and sauté the leek for 5 minutes, or until translucent. Stir in the spinach and season with salt and pepper. Let cool, then form into 2 patties and wrap in plastic wrap.

In a covered steamer over boiling water, steam the fish fillets and the leek and spinach cakes for 5 to 10 minutes, or until the fish is opaque throughout.

Meanwhile, in a medium nonaluminum saucepan, combine the stock and wine and cook over medium heat until the liquid is reduced to 1 cup (8 fl oz/250 ml). Add the cream and cook again to reduce to ¾ cup (6 fl oz/180 ml). Stir in the cucumber and dill and season with salt and pepper.

Place the leek and spinach cakes in the center of each of 2 plates. Place 1 fillet on each plate, spoon some of the sauce over each fillet, and garnish with the fresh herbs.

Makes 4 servings

Gregans Castle

Chocolate Soufflé

Delicious served plain or with whole raspberries, strawberries, or a fresh berry coulis.

1 cup (8 fl oz/250 ml) milk
1 vanilla bean, split lengthwise
2 ounces (60 g) bittersweet chocolate, grated
4 eggs, separated
1½ tablespoons flour
¼ cup (2 oz/60 g) sugar
1 tablespoon butter
Powdered sugar for dusting

Preheat the oven to 400°F (200°C). Butter a 6-cup (48–fl oz/1.5-l) soufflé dish and sprinkle it with sugar.

In a medium saucepan, combine the milk, vanilla bean, and chocolate and bring to a boil over medium-low heat. Set aside.

In a medium bowl, beat 2 of the egg yolks, the flour, and sugar together until pale in color. Gradually whisk the egg mixture into the milk mixture. Cook over medium-low heat until the custard coats the back of a spoon, stirring constantly. Strain through a fine-meshed sieve. Set aside and let cool.

Stir the remaining 2 egg yolks and the butter into the chocolate mixture and mix thoroughly. In a large bowl, beat the egg whites until stiff, glossy peaks form. Carefully fold the egg whites into the chocolate mixture. Pour into the prepared soufflé dish and level off with a palette knife. Bake in the preheated oven for 15 to 20 minutes, or until the soufflé is well risen. Dust with powdered sugar and serve at once.

Makes 4 servings

Hunter's Hotel
Rathnew, County Wicklow

Owned and managed by the Gelletlies, Hunter's Hotel is one of Ireland's oldest coaching inns and has been in the same family for five generations. It was opened by Mrs. Hunter in 1830, who believed that its immediate success was due to "the courtesy and civility of the staff"—a tradition of friendliness and hospitality that is carefully maintained today. The hotel was at that time the first night's stop for the stagecoach out of Dublin on the southern route. In following years, travelers came by train. In the 1920s, cycling clubs visited, and later, groups of serious day-hikers who returned to the hotel in time for a delicious dinner.

Hunter's Hotel offers seventeen charming bedrooms with fireplaces, antique furnishings, and fresh flowers. Guests enjoy fishing, horse riding, tennis, golf, sightseeing, and the beautiful sandy beaches in the vicinity. The picturesque gardens along the banks of the Vartry River provide a haven from the world at large, as well as a delightful setting for an old-fashioned afternoon tea or a drink before dinner.

The dinners served at Hunter's Hotel are still hearty coaching-house meals, the very best of Irish food. The menu highlights fresh seafood, Wicklow lamb and beef, game in season, and vegetables straight from the hotel garden, all cooked with care and attractively presented. Chef John Sutton suggests the following menu for New Year's Eve.

THE MENU
Hunter's Hotel
A New Year's Eve Menu

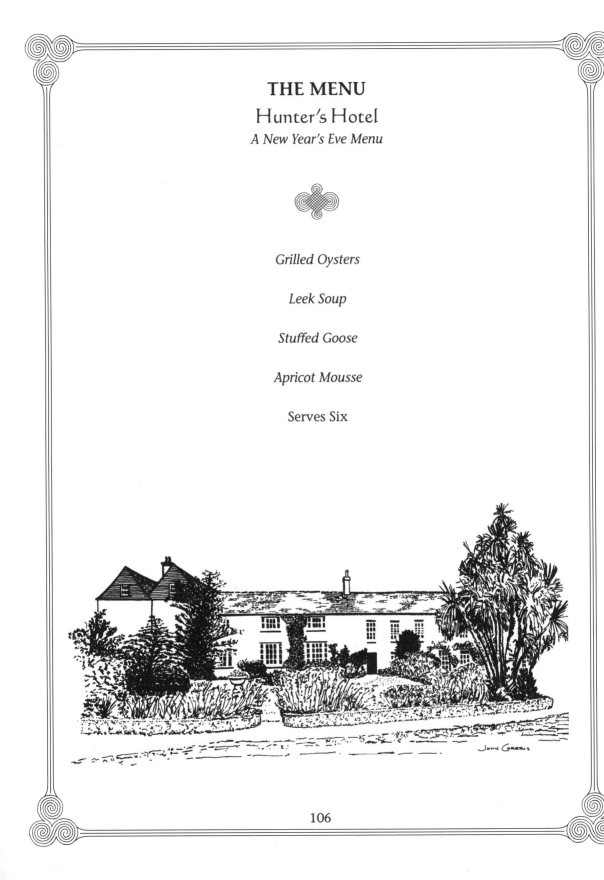

Grilled Oysters

Leek Soup

Stuffed Goose

Apricot Mousse

Serves Six

Grilled Oysters

Serve with lemon wedges, freshly made brown bread and butter, and a glass of Guinness.

24 large oysters in the shell
4 tablespoons (2 oz/60 g) butter, plus butter for serving
2 teaspoons Worcestershire sauce
Salt and freshly ground black pepper to taste
Brown bread for serving (see page 157)
6 lemon wedges

Shuck the oysters. Arrange the oysters in their deeper half shells on a broiler pan.

Preheat the broiler. In a small saucepan over medium heat, melt the 4 tablespoons (2 oz/60 g) butter and stir in the Worcestershire sauce. Pour 1 teaspoon of the sauce over each oyster and season with salt and pepper. Place the pan under the preheated broiler and broil until the oysters begin to curl at the edges. Serve immediately with brown bread and butter. Garnish with lemon wedges.

Makes 6 servings

Leek Soup

3 large leeks
2 tablespoons butter
1 teaspoon olive oil
2 potatoes, peeled and diced
4 cups (32 fl oz/1 l) chicken stock (see page 213) or canned
  low-salt chicken broth
Freshly ground sea salt and black pepper to taste

Trim the leeks at the base and remove the tops of the green leaves. Slit the leeks lengthwise and wash under cold running water, between the layers, to remove any grit. Finely slice and reserve a handful of the leeks for garnish.

In a large, heavy saucepan, melt the butter together with the olive oil over medium heat and sauté the leeks for 5 to 10 minutes, or until tender but not browned. Stir in the potatoes and stock or broth, raise the heat to medium, and bring to a boil. Reduce heat to low and simmer for 20 to 30 minutes, or until the potatoes are tender.

Meanwhile, in a pot of salted boiling water, blanch the reserved leeks for 2 minutes, then drain, rinse under cold water, and drain again.

Transfer the soup to a blender or food processor and purée. Rinse the saucepan, add the purée, and bring just to a boil. Season with salt and pepper, ladle into soup bowls, and garnish with the blanched leeks.

Makes 6 servings

Stuffed Goose

Serve with roasted parsnips and creamed potatoes. If you plan to make traditional brown gravy from the drippings, pour a glass of port over the goose just before the end of the cooking time.

Stuffing

2 tablespoons bacon fat or vegetable oil
2 onions, chopped
1 tablespoon minced fresh sage
4 cups (16 oz/500 g) dried bread crumbs
Salt and freshly ground black pepper to taste
Chicken stock or broth as needed

One 8-pound (4-kg) goose
Fresh lemon juice for rubbing
Salt and freshly ground black pepper to taste

Preheat the oven to 350°F (180°C). To prepare the stuffing: In a large sauté pan or skillet over medium heat, heat the bacon fat or oil and sauté the onions for 5 minutes, or until tender but not browned. Stir in the sage, bread crumbs, salt, and pepper. If the stuffing is too dry, moisten with a little stock or broth.

Spoon the stuffing into the goose crop. Place any excess stuffing in the body cavity. Rub the goose with lemon juice, salt, and pepper. Bake in the preheated oven, basting often, for 2 to 2½ hours, or until a meat thermometer inserted in the thickest part of the thigh registers 175°F to 180°F (80°C to 82°C). Let rest at least 15 minutes before carving.

Makes 6 servings

Apricot Mousse

Start this light dessert the evening before you plan to serve it by soaking the apricots. Serve with Irish coffee (see page 212).

1⅓ cups (8 oz/250 g) dried apricots
Pared zest and juice of ½ lemon
2 apples, peeled, cored, and sliced
½ cup (4 oz/125 g) sugar, or to taste
3 egg whites
½ cup (2 oz/60 g) almonds, toasted (see page 224)

Place the apricots in a bowl, cover with boiling water, and soak overnight.

In a medium saucepan, combine the apricots and their liquid, lemon zest and juice, and apples and cook over medium heat for 10 minutes, or until the apples are very tender. Drain off the liquid and, using a wooden spoon, push the apricot mixture through a fine-meshed sieve or purée in a blender; refrigerate until chilled. Add the sugar to the purée and stir until well blended.

In a large bowl, beat the egg whites until stiff, glossy peaks form. Fold the egg whites into the apricot mixture until evenly blended and spoon the mousse into 4 individual glasses. Sprinkle with toasted almonds and serve.

Makes 4 servings

Kildare Hotel & Country Club
Straffan, County Kildare

Now renamed the Kildare Hotel & Country Club, the former Straffan House dates back at least to the Anglo-Norman invasion of Ireland, when it was given by Strongbow to Maurice Fitzgerald, an ancestor of the dukes of Leinster. This grant was subsequently confirmed by Richard the Lionhearted's brother, who became King John of England. The property was held by prominent titled families from the sixteenth through the nineteenth centuries, and was sold to Hugh Barton in 1831. Straffan House remained in the Barton family until 1949 and was eventually sold; it opened its doors as the Kildare, a luxury hotel and country club, in 1991.

The old country house has been transformed into a magnificent five-star hotel that has won international acclaim. Just seventeen miles from Dublin, the Kildare is set amid acres of spacious lawns and woodlands overlooking the River Liffey. Elegant reception rooms are furnished with antiques and master paintings, and the hotel's forty-five bedrooms and suites are splendidly luxurious. Guests and club members choose from a wide range of recreational activities, including golf, croquet, lake and river fishing, clay pigeon shooting, horse riding, and indoor tennis or squash.

The Byerley Turk restaurant is a superb setting for chef Michel Flamme's evening meals. His menu blends classical French and Irish cuisine and is complemented by a carefully chosen wine list. The Legend's Room in the golf club is ideal for less formal dining. The following dinner menu was created for Menus and Music by Michel Flamme.

THE MENU
Kildare Hotel & Country Club

Millefeuille of Mushrooms and Spinach with Armagnac Cream

Cauliflower and Cumin Soup

Panfried Noisettes of Beef with Ratatouille and Shallot Sabayon

Caramel Mousse

Serves Four

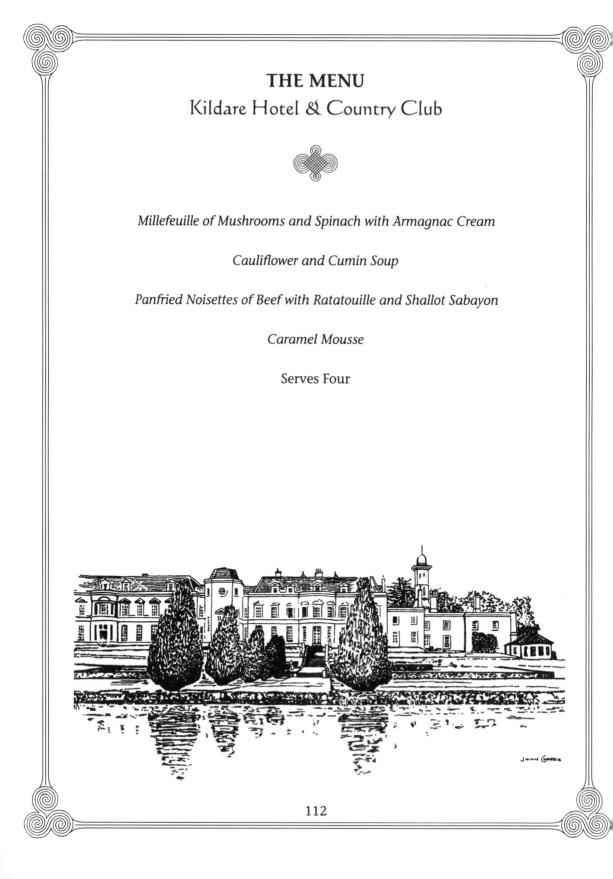

Millefeuille of Mushrooms and Spinach with Armagnac Cream

An absolutely elegant first course for a special dinner.

Two 12-by-17-inch (30-by-43-cm) filo sheets
⅓ cup (3 oz/90 g) butter, melted
2 tablespoons sesame seeds for sprinkling

Armagnac Cream
2¼ cups (18 fl oz/560 ml) reduced chicken stock or
   canned low-salt chicken broth (see page 223)
2 cups (16 fl oz/500 ml) heavy (whipping) cream
½ cup (4 oz/125 g) butter, cut into small pieces
Salt and freshly ground black pepper to taste
Minced fresh chervil to taste
½ cup (4 fl oz/125 ml) Armagnac

8 ounces (250 g) baby spinach leaves, blanched, squeezed dry,
   and chopped
¼ cup (2 fl oz/60 ml) heavy (whipping) cream
4 tablespoons (2 oz/60 g) butter
6 ounces (185 g) cèpe (porcini) mushrooms
3 ounces (90 g) girolle mushrooms
8 ounces (250 g) shiitake mushrooms, stemmed
8 ounces (250 g) oyster mushrooms
8 ounces (250 g) field (crimini) mushrooms
1 garlic clove, crushed
Minced fresh parsley
Salt and freshly ground black pepper to taste

Preheat the oven to 325°F (165°C). Place 1 filo sheet on a work surface and brush lightly with half of the butter. Top with the second filo sheet and brush with the remaining butter and sprinkle lightly with sesame seeds. Using a 4-inch (10-cm) round cookie cutter, cut the filo into 12 disks. Bake the filo disks in the preheated oven for 8 to 10 minutes, or until golden brown.

To make the Armagnac cream: In a medium saucepan, cook the stock or broth over high heat to reduce to 3 tablespoons. Add the cream and cook until thick enough to coat the back of a spoon. Gradually whisk in the butter in pieces until incorporated. Stir in the salt, pepper, and chervil, then the Armagnac. Set aside and keep warm.

In a small nonaluminum saucepan, combine the spinach and the cream and cook over medium heat for 2 minutes; set aside and keep warm. In a large sauté pan or skillet, melt the butter over medium-high heat and sauté the mushrooms for 2 minutes, or until browned, in batches if necessary. Add the garlic and parsley and cook 2 minutes more; remove from heat. Season with salt and pepper.

Arrange the millefeuilles as follows: Spread the spinach on 4 filo disks and top each with another disk of filo. Spread these with the mushroom mixture and top each with a disk of filo. Pour some of the Armagnac cream around the plate and serve immediately.

Makes 4 servings

Kildare Hotel & Country Club

Cauliflower and Cumin Soup

1 cauliflower, cut into florets
1½ teaspoons cumin seed
⅓ cup (3 oz/90 g) butter
2 cups (16 fl oz/500 ml) milk
2 cups (16 fl oz/500 ml) heavy (whipping) cream
Salt and freshly ground black pepper to taste

In a large saucepan, combine all the ingredients and simmer over medium-low heat for 20 minutes. Transfer to a blender or food processor and purée. Adjust the seasoning and serve warm.

Makes 4 servings

Panfried Noisettes of Beef with Ratatouille and Shallot Sabayon

Although there are several stages to this recipe, they are not difficult.

Ratatouille

3 tablespoons olive oil

2 small onions, chopped

1 small eggplant, finely diced

2 small zucchini, finely diced

1 small green bell pepper, seeded, deribbed, and finely diced

1 small red bell pepper, seeded, deribbed, and finely diced

2 garlic cloves, minced

1 bouquet garni: 3 fresh parsley sprigs, 2 fresh thyme sprigs,
    and 1 bay leaf tied in a cheesecloth bag

Shallot Sabayon

2 tablespoons butter

20 shallots, minced

½ cup (4 fl oz/125 ml) chicken stock or
    canned low-salt chicken broth

1 cup (8 fl oz/250 ml) heavy (whipping) cream

6 egg yolks

1 tablespoon olive oil

8 crosswise slices fillet of beef (3½ oz/100 g each)

To make the ratatouille: In a large, heavy pot over medium heat, heat the olive oil and sauté the onions until translucent, about 5 minutes. Stir in the eggplant and zucchini and sauté until browned. Add the peppers, garlic, and bouquet garni and cook until the peppers are tender.

To make the shallot sabayon: In a large sauté pan or skillet, melt the butter over medium-low heat and sauté the shallots for 5 minutes, or until tender but not browned; set aside.

In a medium saucepan, cook the stock or broth over high heat until reduced by half. Whisk in the cream and egg yolks, reduce heat to medium low, and cook until thick enough to coat the back of a spoon; do not let boil. Stir in the shallots.

Preheat the broiler. In a large sauté pan or skillet over medium-high heat, heat the oil and fry the fillet slices to your taste. Arrange 2 slices on each of 4 heatproof plates and top with warm ratatouille and some shallot sabayon. Broil the fillets under the preheated broiler for 1 or 2 minutes, or until the shallot sabayon is browned.

Makes 4 servings

Caramel Mousse

⅞ cup (7 oz/215 g) sugar
¼ cup (2 fl oz/60 ml) fresh lemon juice
1¼ cups (10 fl oz/310 ml) water
1 envelope plain gelatin
5 egg yolks
1 teaspoon milk
1 cup (8 fl oz/250 ml) heavy (whipping) cream

In a medium, heavy saucepan, bring the sugar, lemon juice, and 1cup (8 fl oz/250 ml) water to a boil over medium heat, stirring to dissolve the sugar. Reduce heat to low and cook the syrup until it is golden brown, watching carefully to see that it does not burn; remove from heat.

Pour the remaining ¼ cup (2 fl oz/60 ml) water into a cup and sprinkle the gelatin over. Let sit for 5 minutes. In a small bowl, whisk together the egg yolks and milk. Stir the yolk mixture and gelatin mixture into the caramel. Let cool. In a deep bowl, beat the cream until stiff peaks form. Fold the whipped cream into the caramel mixture and spoon the mousse into 4 glasses. Refrigerate for at least 6 hours, or until ready to serve.

Makes 4 servings

Longueville House

Mallow, County Cork

Longueville House is a grand Georgian mansion overlooking the Blackwater Valley, one of the most beautiful river valleys in Ireland. Built in 1720, the home's background reflects the history of Ireland: The lands, originally owned by the O'Callaghan family, were seized by Cromwell and given to Baron Longueville, who built the house; both house and lands were then later bought back by Senator William O'Callaghan in 1938. Michael and Jane O'Callaghan have owned and managed Longueville since 1967, and today they run the elegant country house hotel with their son William.

The impressive view from the house takes in the ruins of Dromineen Castle, the ancient seat of the O'Callaghans, and the Blackwater River forms a boundary of the five-hundred-acre wooded estate and farm. Longueville has an impressive stone entrance hall, beautiful Regency plasterwork, and a fine Turner conservatory. The twenty comfortable guest bedrooms are decorated with antique furnishings. In the superb Presidents' Restaurant, with its commissioned portraits of Ireland's past presidents and its graceful Adam mantlepiece, you can taste a glass of O'Callaghan white wine (the vineyard on the grounds is the only one in Ireland!).

The heart of Longueville, the Presidents' Restaurant, is presided over by William O'Callaghan, an exceptionally talented chef who is dedicated to excellence and immersed in developing Irish cuisine. His creative seasonal menus feature ingredients from Longueville's working farm, kitchen garden, and stretch of the Blackwater River—the Longueville estate is almost completely self-sufficient. An international list of carefully chosen wines complement the menu. William O'Callaghan created the following recipes for Menus and Music.

THE MENU
Longueville House

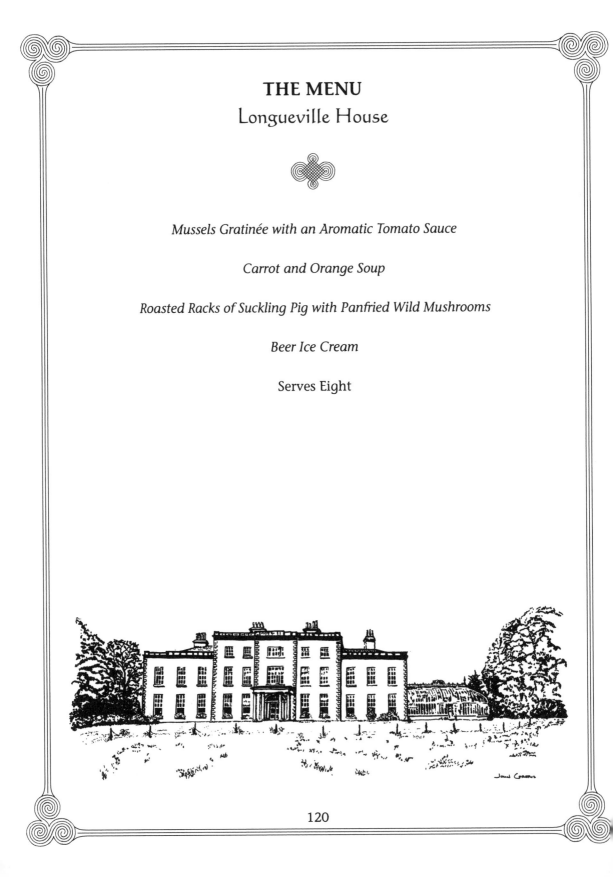

Mussels Gratinée with an Aromatic Tomato Sauce

Carrot and Orange Soup

Roasted Racks of Suckling Pig with Panfried Wild Mushrooms

Beer Ice Cream

Serves Eight

Mussels Gratinée with an Aromatic Tomato Sauce

Mussels are plentiful along the coast of Ireland and are often used in soups and chowders. In this appetizer, their delicate sea flavor is highlighted by an outstanding tomato sauce flavored with fennel, thyme, and star anise.

Mussels

2 tablespoons butter

½ onion, chopped

1 carrot, peeled and chopped

1 fresh parsley sprig

1 fresh thyme sprig

7 pounds (3.5 kg) mussels, scrubbed and debearded

½ cup (4 fl oz/125 ml) dry white wine

Salt and freshly ground pepper to taste

Bread Crumbs

4 stale bread slices, broken up

Leaves from 1 fresh thyme sprig

2 tablespoons minced fresh parsley

Leaves from 1 fresh rosemary sprig

Leaves from 1 fresh fennel frond

1½ tablespoons olive oil

Tomato Sauce

2 tablespoons olive oil

1 onion, chopped

½ fennel bulb, chopped

6 tomatoes, seeded (see page 220)

1 fresh thyme sprig

1 star anise pod

Reserved mussel stock

Salt and freshly ground black pepper to taste

Butter 8 shallow heatproof ramekins. In a large sauté pan or skillet, melt the butter over medium-low heat and sauté the onion, carrot, parsley,

121

and thyme until the onion is translucent, about 5 minutes. Add the mussels and white wine and cover the pan with a lid. Shake the pan occasionally and cook until all the shells have opened, about 5 minutes; remove from heat.

Using a slotted spoon, transfer the mussels to a plate; reserve the mussel stock. Remove the mussels from the shells and set the mussels aside.

To make the bread crumbs: In a blender or food processor, grind all the ingredients together.

To make the tomato sauce: In a large sauté pan or skillet over medium heat, heat the olive oil and sauté the onion and fennel until the onion is translucent, about 5 minutes. Stir in the tomatoes, thyme, star anise, and reserved mussel stock and simmer for 15 minutes. Remove the anise pod and thyme sprig and season with salt and pepper.

Preheat the broiler. Place the prepared molds on a broiler pan. Season the warm mussels with salt and pepper and pack them into the ramekins. Top with the bread crumbs.

Broil in the preheated broiler until the bread crumbs are golden brown; remove from heat. Unmold in the center of each of 8 salad plates, surround with the tomato sauce, and serve immediately.

Makes 8 servings

Carrot and Orange Soup

Vegetable Stock
1 tablespoon olive oil
2 carrots, peeled and chopped
3 onions, chopped
2 garlic cloves, minced
3 leeks, chopped

3 celery stalks, chopped
1 tablespoon olive oil
10 carrots, peeled and chopped
1 onion, chopped
2 potatoes, peeled and chopped
1 fresh tarragon sprig
Grated zest of ¼ orange
Salt and freshly ground black pepper to taste
Fresh lemon juice to taste
1 tablespoon minced fresh parsley

To make the vegetable stock: In a large saucepan over medium-low heat, heat the olive oil and sauté the carrots, onions, garlic, leeks, and celery until the onion is translucent, about 7 minutes. Add water to cover the vegetables, raise heat to high, and bring to a boil. Reduce heat to medium and simmer for 20 minutes. Remove from heat and strain through a fine-meshed sieve; reserve the vegetable stock.

In a large sauté pan or skillet over medium-low heat, heat the olive oil and sauté the carrots, onion, potatoes, tarragon, and orange zest for 20 minutes with a lid on; the vegetables should be very soft. Add the vegetable stock and simmer for 30 minutes. Transfer to a blender or food processor, in batches if necessary, and purée. Strain through a fine-meshed sieve. Season the soup with salt, pepper, and lemon juice. Ladle the soup into 8 shallow soup bowls and garnish with the parsley.

Makes 8 servings

Longueville House

Roasted Racks of Suckling Pig
with Panfried Wild Mushrooms

Chef William O'Callaghan serves this dish with homemade tagliatelle.

2 racks from a 28- to 34-pound (14- to 17-kg) suckling pig
3 onions, chopped
3 celery stalks, chopped
2 carrots, peeled and chopped
1 fresh thyme sprig
1 garlic clove, crushed
2 cups (16 fl oz/500 ml) dry white wine
2 cups (16 fl oz/500 ml) veal stock (see page 225) or
    canned low-salt chicken broth
2 cups (16 fl oz/500 ml) chicken stock (see page 213) or
    canned low-salt chicken broth
2 pounds (1 kg) mixed wild mushrooms such as chanterelles,
    cèpes (porcini), oysters, and hedgehogs
2 tablespoons butter
1 tablespoon minced shallot
Salt and freshly ground black pepper to taste
Fresh lemon juice to taste
2 tablespoons olive oil
1 tablespoon minced fresh parsley

To prepare the rack of suckling pig: Trim off 2 inches (5 cm) of the flap. Clean the bones of the 2 racks. When this is complete, divide the racks down the center. Remove the central spine bone from the meat so all that remains is the eye of the loin with the rib bones attached. The rib bones can be cut to the same size with a chopping knife or kitchen scissors, as they are very tender. Better still, ask your butcher to do it for you. Reserve all the bones and roughly chop them.

Preheat the oven to 450°F (230°C). Arrange the reserved bones in a baking pan filmed with vegetable oil and bake until almost brown, about 30 minutes.

Longueville House

Add the onions, celery, carrots, thyme, and garlic and cook until the bones and vegetables are browned, about 30 minutes. Transfer the bones and vegetables to a large stockpot or saucepan. Pour off the fat in the baking pan and place the pan over medium heat. Add the white wine, stirring to scrape up the browned bits from the bottom of the pan. Bring the liquid to a boil and reduce it by a third. Transfer the liquid to the large saucepan and add the stock or broth. Bring to the boil, reduce heat to low, and simmer for 1 hour. Strain the stock through a fine-meshed sieve.

To prepare the mushrooms: Stem them, reserving the tops, and chop the stems. In a large sauté pan or skillet, melt 1 tablespoon of the butter over medium heat and sauté the shallot for 2 minutes. Add the chopped stems, reduce heat to low, and cook for another 3 minutes. Add the stock and simmer for 20 minutes. Transfer to a blender or food processor and purée. Strain through a fine-meshed sieve. Season with salt, pepper, and lemon juice to taste.

To cook the meat: Season the racks of pork with salt and pepper. Preheat the oven to 350°F (180°C). In a large, heavy ovenproof skillet over high heat, heat 1 tablespoon of the oil and sear the seasoned racks of pork for 4 minutes on each side. Place the pan in the bottom of the preheated oven and bake, skin-side down, for 15 to 20 minutes, or until a meat thermometer reads 185°F (85°C). Remove the meat from the oven and, using a sharp knife, take the skin off the rack. Remove the fat from the skin. Keep the racks in a warm place. Cut the skin into slices and broil it, or put it back into the oven until the skin turns into cracklings. Reserve any of the cooking juices and add them to the sauce.

In a large sauté pan or skillet over high heat, melt the remaining 1 tablespoon butter with the remaining 1 tablespoon oil and sauté the reserved whole mushrooms for 5 minutes. Sprinkle with the parsley and add salt, pepper, and lemon juice to taste.

Carve the racks into cutlets. Arrange a bed of mushrooms on each of 8 plates and top with the pork cutlets. Spoon the mushroom sauce over and serve immediately.

Makes 8 servings

Longueville House

Beer Ice Cream

Beer cuts the sweetness of sugar and cream and makes for a delicious and unusual ice cream flavor.

3 cups (24 fl oz/750 ml) heavy (whipping) cream
1½ cups (12 fl oz/375 ml) lager (pale beer)
1 cup (8 oz/250 g) sugar
12 egg yolks

In a large, heavy saucepan, combine the cream, beer, and ¾ cup (6 oz/190 g) of the sugar. Cook over medium-low heat, stirring constantly, until the mixture comes to a boil. Remove from heat.

In a medium bowl, beat the egg yolks and the remaining ¼ cup (2 oz/60 g) sugar together until pale in color. Add the egg mixture to the cream mixture and cook over low heat for 3 minutes.

Let cool and freeze in an ice cream maker according to the manufacturer's instructions.

Makes about 2 quarts

Longueville House

Marlfield House

Gorey, County Wexford

Originally built as a Regency-style mansion in 1820 for the Earl of Courtown, Marlfield House has been lovingly transformed into an exquisite country house hotel by Mary and Raymond Bowe. It offers a splendidly opulent retreat with a blend of warmth and character. The thirteen luxurious bedrooms and six apartments, each one individually designed by Mary Bowe, are adorned with marble fireplaces, ornate plasterwork, magnificent antiques, sumptuous fabrics, and flowers, and feature palatial bathrooms. Guests can enjoy a drink while studying the menu and wine list in the bar, or read in the drawing room in front of a log fire. This elegant country house has been chosen twice by the Hideaway Report as one of the Best Twenty-Five Hotels in the World; is a member of Relais & Chateaux; and has received the Bord Fáilte Award for Excellence for its restaurant eight years running.

Marlfield is nestled in a thirty-five-acre estate of woodlands and extensive landscaped gardens. The property also includes an ornamental lake for Mary's pet ducks, and Ray's carefully tended kitchen gardens, which supply fresh vegetables, fruits, and herbs for the kitchen.

Marlfield's bountiful breakfasts include porridge, eggs, smoked bacon, sausages, traditional black and white puddings, Irish cheeses, and fresh-baked scones and breads. In the formal dining room, carefully overseen by Mary Bowe, guests enjoy a sumptuous dining experience. Expertly cooked dishes are graciously served in the lovely Victorian conservatory, and an outstanding selection of wines from the cellar complement the menu. Chef Kevin Arundel created the following dinner menu for Menus and Music.

THE MENU
Marlfield House

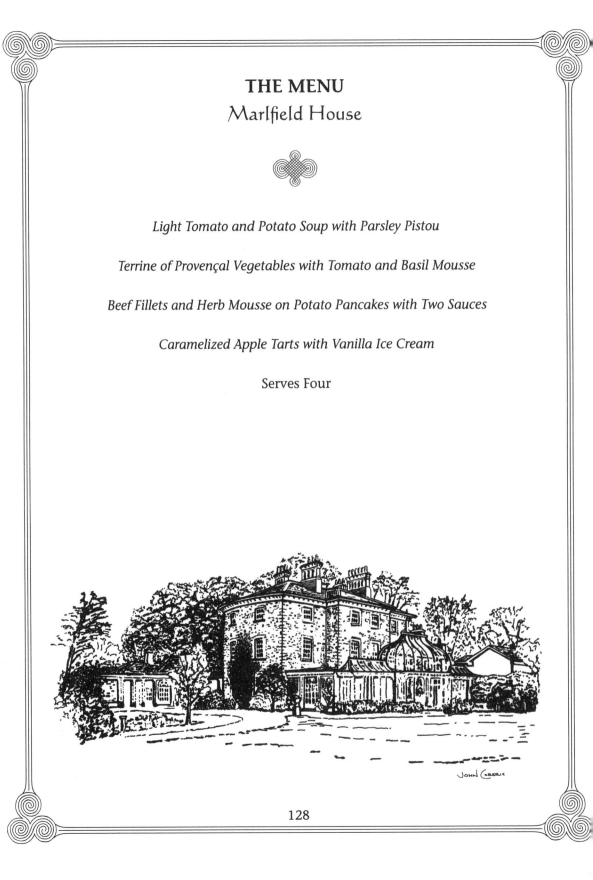

Light Tomato and Potato Soup with Parsley Pistou

Terrine of Provençal Vegetables with Tomato and Basil Mousse

Beef Fillets and Herb Mousse on Potato Pancakes with Two Sauces

Caramelized Apple Tarts with Vanilla Ice Cream

Serves Four

Light Tomato and Potato Soup with Parsley Pistou

This soup is a summer treat that is most flavorful if you use garden-fresh tomatoes.

2 tablespoons butter
1 onion
1 leek
7 tomatoes, chopped
3 potatoes
3 cups (24 fl oz/750 ml) water
Salt and freshly ground black pepper to taste

Parsley Pistou
1 garlic clove
1 cup (1½ oz/45 g) minced fresh parsley
¼ cup (2 fl oz/60 ml) olive oil
¼ teaspoon salt
2 tablespoons water

2 tablespoons butter, cut into small pieces
¼ cup (2 fl oz/60 ml) heavy (whipping) cream (optional)

In a large saucepan over low heat, melt the butter and sauté the onions and leeks for 5 minutes, or until translucent but not browned. Stir in the tomatoes. Add the potatoes and water and simmer until the potatoes are tender, about 20 minutes. Transfer to a blender or food processor and purée. Strain through a fine-meshed sieve back into a clean saucepan. Season with salt and pepper.

To make the parsley pistou: In a blender or food processor, purée the garlic cloves, parsley, olive oil, salt, and water.

Heat the soup and gradually whisk in the butter and the cream, if using. (Boil the cream first so it will not curdle with the acid of the tomatoes.) Ladle the soup into 4 shallow bowls, place 1 tablespoon parsley pistou in the center of each bowl, and serve immediately.

Makes 4 servings

Terrine of Provençal Vegetables with Tomato and Basil Mousse

A tasty vegetarian terrine wrapped in a spinach envelope.

Mousse
½ tablespoon olive oil

1 shallot

1 garlic clove

¼ cup (1½ fl oz/45 ml) canned chopped tomatoes

5 fresh tomatoes, peeled and seeded (see page 220)

½ tablespoon tomato paste

2 tablespoons dry white wine

3 fresh basil leaves

Salt and freshly ground black pepper to taste

2 tablespoons water

½ envelope (½ tablespoon) plain gelatin

Filling
3 zucchini, quartered lengthwise

1 red bell pepper

1 green bell pepper

1 tablespoon olive oil

Salt and freshly ground black pepper to taste

1 small eggplant

1 fennel bulb, trimmed and halved lengthwise

10 large spinach leaves, blanched and seasoned to
   taste with salt and pepper

To make the mousse: In a large saucepan over medium-low heat, heat the olive oil and sauté the shallot and garlic for 3 minutes. Add the canned tomatoes and cook for 5 to 10 minutes over medium heat. Add the fresh tomatoes and cook until tender. Cook until reduced to taste, then add the tomato purée and the wine and reduce to taste again. Add the basil leaves and simmer for

5 minutes. Meanwhile, pour the water into a cup and sprinkle the gelatin over. Let sit for 5 minutes. Stir into the mousse mixture. Purée the mousse mixture in a blender and strain it through a fine-meshed sieve. Taste and adjust the seasoning.

To make the filling: Preheat the oven to 475°F (245°C). In a large pot of boiling water, blanch the zucchini for 2 minutes, then drain and plunge into ice water. Film a baking sheet with vegetable oil, halve the red and green peppers lengthwise, and bake for 10 minutes. Place the peppers in a covered pot until cool to the touch, then peel, seed, and dice them finely.

Cut the eggplant into long ¼-inch-thick (6-mm) strips with skin on one side (reserve the remaining eggplant for another use). In a sauté pan over medium-low heat, heat the olive oil and sauté the peppers for 2 minutes. Season with salt and pepper. Using a slotted spoon, transfer to paper towels to drain. Sauté the eggplant strips for 3 to 4 minutes. Season with salt and pepper and, using a slotted spoon, transfer to paper towels to drain. Sauté the fennel until crisp-tender, 3 to 4 minutes. Season with salt and pepper and transfer to paper towels to drain.

Line a terrine with the spinach leaves, allowing ends to hang over the edge of the terrine. Pour in half of the tomato-basil mousse, add the filling, and top with the remaining mousse. Fold the spinach leaves over the contents to enclose them.

Makes 4 servings

Beef Fillets and Herb Mousse on Potato Pancakes with Two Sauces

4 tablespoons (2 fl oz/60 ml) clarified butter (see page 214)

20 shallots

Salt and freshly ground black pepper to taste

1 tablespoon olive oil

Four 7-ounce (220-g) beef fillet steaks

1 tablespoon minced mixed fresh herbs such as basil, tarragon, and chives

¼ cup (2 oz/60 g) pâté de foie gras

½ ounce (15 g) caul fat*, cut into 4 squares

2 large potatoes

Four 4-inch (10-cm) Potato Pancakes (recipe follows)

½ cup (4 fl oz/125 ml) Mustard Seed Butter Sauce (see page 213)

½ cup (4 fl oz/125 ml) Red Wine Sauce (see page 222)

In a large sauté pan or skillet over low heat, heat the butter and cook the shallots, stirring occasionally, for 20 minutes, or until tender and caramelized.

Meanwhile, preheat the oven to 350°F (180°C). In a large sauté pan or skillet over high heat, heat the oil and sear the steaks on both sides until lightly browned. Remove from the pan, season with salt and pepper, and let cool. Blend the herbs into the pâté. Mound one-fourth of the mixture on top of each slice of beef in a smooth dome. Place a square of caul fat over each mound. Place the steaks in a roasting pan and bake in the preheated oven for 10 minutes. Remove from the oven and let sit for 5 minutes.

Place a potato pancake on each of 4 warm plates and top with steak. Surround with shallots, pour one of the sauces on either side of each plate, and serve.

Makes 4 servings

*Caul fat is available from butchers.

Potato Pancakes

1 potato, peeled and chopped

1 teaspoon milk

1 teaspoon flour

1 egg

1 teaspoon heavy (whipping) cream

2 tablespoons butter

1 tablespoon olive oil

In a medium saucepan of salted boiling water, cook the potato until tender, about 15 minutes. Drain and transfer to a blender or food processor. Add the milk and purée. Let cool and then blend in the flour, egg, and cream.

In a large sauté pan or skillet over medium heat, melt the butter with the olive oil. Spoon the batter into the pan by fourths and cook the pancakes until golden on both sides.

Makes 4 small pancakes

Caramelized Apple Tarts with Vanilla Ice Cream

2 sheets puff pastry

1 egg

¼ cup (2 oz/60 g)plus 1 tablespoon sugar

¾ cup (4 oz/125 g) almonds, ground

1 tablespoon Calvados or brandy

Juice of ½ lemon

4 tablespoons (2 oz/60 g) butter, cut into tablespoon-sized pieces

4 scoops vanilla ice cream

4 apples, peeled, quartered, and cored

Preheat the oven to 475°F (245°C) for at least 15 minutes.

Cut the puff pastry into eight 5½-inch (14-cm) disks. Place 4 disks on a baking sheet. Beat the egg and 1 tablespoon of the sugar together and brush the disks with the egg mixture. Cut 4½-inch (11-cm) disks from the remaining 4 disks and place the resulting rings on top of the first 4 disks as neatly as possible. Sprinkle one-fourth of the ground almonds over each one.

In a small saucepan, combine the remaining ¼ cup (2 oz/60 g) sugar, Calvados or brandy, and lemon juice and bring to a boil. Whisk in the butter one piece at a time until incorporated; set aside.

Cut each apple quarter into 5 slices and fan them neatly inside each prepared tart, using 1 apple for each tart. Brush with some of the syrup. Bake in the preheated oven for 10 minutes, then brush with more syrup and bake for another 5 minutes, or until the pastry is browned and the apples are tender. Serve each tart with a scoop of vanilla ice cream.

Makes 4 individual tarts

Newport House
Newport, County Mayo

A stately vine-covered mansion overlooking the Newport River and quay, Newport House was built in the mid-1700s as the home of the O'Donel family. Today the grand Georgian-style house is a peaceful retreat that offers elegance, comfort, and relaxation in beautiful County Mayo. It is especially beloved by fishing enthusiasts, who enjoy salmon and sea trout fishing on the Newport River, Lough Beltra, and other bountiful freshwater lakes and streams in the vicinity. Many guests are anglers who come back year after year for the excellent fishing and luxurious surroundings.

More like an old-fashioned gentleman's club than a hotel, Newport House offers comfortable and spacious guest rooms: twelve in the main house and six others in two smaller houses near the courtyard (one of which was previously the holiday residence of the late Sean Lemass, prime minister of Ireland). The sensitive restoration of the building, which features wedding-cake plasterwork and a graceful skylighted staircase, was completed in 1987 by proprietors Thelma and Kieran Thompson. They have lovingly furnished the house with elegant period furniture, Regency-style mirrors, and appropriate fixtures. (Kieran was himself a fishing guest at Newport House, and bought it in 1985 so that he could indulge in his favorite pastime as often as he wanted!) Newport House is a member of Relais & Chateaux.

In the dining room, chef John Gavin's splendid cooking reflects the hospitable character of the house and "allows the quality of the food to come out." Of course the menu highlights fresh fish and Newport's legendary home-smoked salmon, and there is outstanding fresh produce from the estate's walled organic kitchen garden, which has been worked since 1720. The cellar offers an extensive international selection with many classic vintages.

THE MENU
Newport House

Avocado Mousse Wrapped in Smoked Salmon with Tomato Coulis

Leek and Potato Soup

Grilled Salmon with Sorrel Sauce

Pineapple and Nectarine Timbales with Banana-Rum Ice Cream

Serves Four

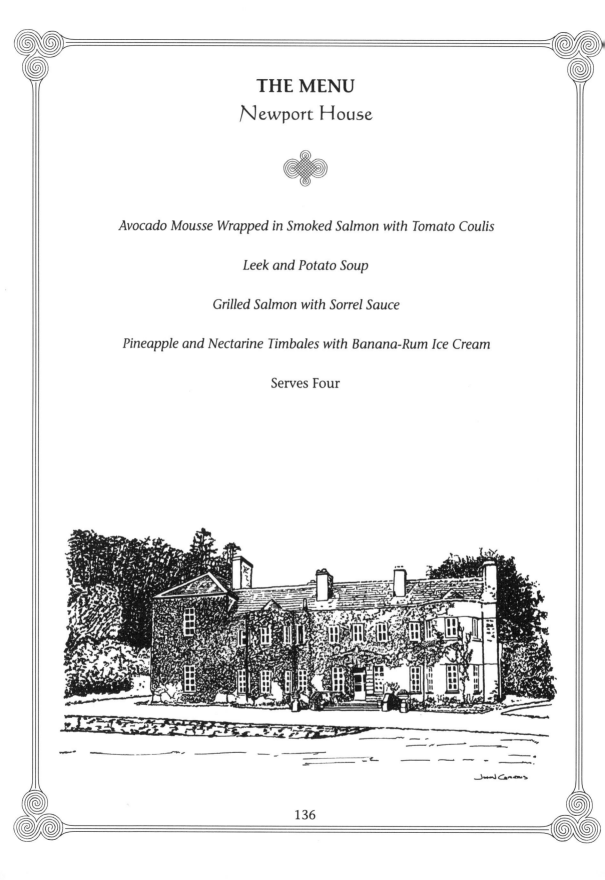

Avocado Mousse Wrapped in Smoked Salmon with Tomato Coulis

This mousse is beautiful, and its taste is sublime.

16 slices smoked salmon
¼ cup (2 fl oz/60 ml) water
1 envelope plain gelatin
2 avocados, peeled, pitted, and puréed
¾ cup (6 fl oz/180 ml) heavy (whipping) cream
3 teaspoons fresh lemon juice
3 teaspoons walnut oil
1 teaspoon Tabasco or to taste
Salt and freshly ground black pepper to taste
Avocado slices for garnish
Fresh chervil sprigs for garnish
Tomato Coulis (recipe follows)

Line a 4-cup (32–fl oz/1-l) terrine with plastic wrap. Line the terrine with slices of smoked salmon, letting them overlap the edges. Refrigerate.

To make the avocado mousse: Pour the water into a cup and sprinkle the gelatin over. Let sit for 5 minutes. Mix the gelatin mixture into the avocado purée. In a deep bowl, beat the cream until soft peaks form. Gently fold the whipped cream, lemon juice, walnut oil, Tabasco, salt, and pepper into the avocado mixture.

Spoon the mousse into the prepared terrine and fold the slices of smoked salmon over it. Refrigerate for 1½ to 2 hours.

Just before serving, slice the terrine with a large knife that has been dipped in hot water. Garnish each slice with avocado slices, chervil sprigs, and some tomato coulis.

Makes 4 servings

Tomato Coulis

3 tablespoons butter
¼ cup (1 oz/30 g) minced shallots
1 garlic clove
1 pinch *each* minced fresh thyme, sage, and rosemary
2 pounds (1 kg) ripe tomatoes, peeled and seeded (see page 220)
Salt and freshly ground black pepper to taste
Sugar to taste

In a medium, heavy saucepan, melt the butter and sauté the shallots and garlic for 3 to 4 minutes, or until translucent. Stir in the thyme, sage, rosemary, and tomatoes and simmer for 8 to 10 minutes. Transfer to a blender or food processor and purée. Strain through a fine-meshed sieve into a large nonaluminum saucepan. Bring to a boil. Remove from heat and season with salt, pepper, and sugar to taste.

Makes about 3 cups (24 fl oz/750 ml)

Leek and Potato Soup

4 tablespoons (2 oz/60 g) butter

1¼ pounds (625 g) leeks, cleaned and sliced (white part only)

1 cup (4 oz/125 g) chopped onion

¾ cup (3 oz/90 g) chopped celery

4 cups (32 fl oz/1 l) chicken stock (see page 213) or
   canned low-salt chicken broth

8 to 10 ounces (250 to 315 g) potatoes, peeled and chopped

Leaves from 1 sprig fresh thyme

1 fresh sage leaf

Salt and freshly ground black pepper to taste

½ cup (4 fl oz/125 ml) heavy (whipping) cream

In a large saucepan over medium-low heat, melt the butter and sauté the leeks, onion, and celery until the onion is translucent, about 7 minutes; do not allow the vegetables to brown. Add the stock or broth, potatoes, thyme, and sage. Simmer for 20 minutes, or until the vegetables are tender. Transfer to a blender or food processor and purée. Season with salt and pepper and strain through a fine-meshed sieve into a saucepan. Stir in the cream and serve.

Makes 4 servings

Grilled Salmon with Sorrel Sauce

Salmon is the king of fish in Ireland. It figures in many legends and was the main dish served at royal banquets, where it was cooked on a spit after being rubbed with salt and basted with butter and honey. Wild salmon appears regularly on the menu at Newport House.

Sorrel Sauce
2 tablespoons butter
¼ cup (2 fl oz/60 ml) dry vermouth
¼ cup (2 fl oz/60 ml) dry white wine
¼ cup (1 oz/30 g) minced shallots
2 cups (16 fl oz/500 ml) fish stock (see page 217)
½ cup (4 fl oz/125 ml) heavy (whipping) cream
Juice of 1 lemon
Salt and freshly ground black pepper to taste
2 cups (2 oz/60 g) gently packed fresh sorrel leaves, shredded

4 salmon fillets
Olive oil for brushing
Salt and freshly ground black pepper to taste
Fresh chervil sprigs for garnish

To make the sorrel sauce: In a medium saucepan, melt the butter over medium heat and stir in the vermouth, white wine, and shallots. Raise heat to high and cook to reduce the liquid by two-thirds. Stir in the stock and cook to reduce the liquid again by two-thirds. Stir in the cream, lemon juice, salt, and pepper, and cook until the sauce coats the back of a spoon. Strain through a fine-meshed sieve into a saucepan and stir in the sorrel. Keep warm until serving.

Light a charcoal fire in a grill. Brush the salmon fillets lightly with oil and sprinkle with salt and pepper. When the coals are medium-hot, place the fillets on the grill and cook for 2 or 3 minutes on each side, or until opaque on the outside and slightly translucent at the center. Transfer the salmon to 4 warm plates. Spoon the sorrel sauce over, garnish with sprigs of chervil, and serve immediately.

Makes 4 servings

Pineapple and Nectarine Timbales
with Banana-Rum Ice Cream

Caramel cages top this sensational dessert.

Banana-Rum Ice Cream
2 eggs
⅓ cup (3 oz/90 g) sugar
3 tablespoons honey
2 bananas, mashed
Juice of ½ lemon
1 cup (8 fl oz/250 ml) milk
2 cups (16 fl oz/500 ml) heavy (whipping) cream
3 tablespoons dark rum

Vanilla Sauce (recipe follows)
4 pineapple rings
2 fresh nectarines, halved and pitted
4 caramel cages (recipe follows)
Raspberry Coulis (see page 151)

To make the ice cream: In a large bowl, beat the eggs until well blended. Beat in the sugar and honey until smooth and light. Stir in the remaining ingredients. Pour into an ice cream maker and freeze according to the manufacturer's instructions.

Pour a pool of vanilla sauce on each of 4 dessert plates. Arrange a pineapple ring in the center of each of 4 plates. Place a nectarine half, hollow-side up, in the center of each pineapple ring. Place a scoop of banana-rum ice cream in the center of each nectarine. Carefully arrange a caramel cage over. Dot the vanilla sauce in 6 or 7 places with raspberry coulis and run a small knife through the coulis to form hearts.

Makes 4 servings

Vanilla Sauce
2 cups (16 fl oz/500 ml) milk
½ vanilla bean, split lengthwise
6 egg yolks
6 tablespoons (3 oz/90 g) sugar

In a medium, heavy saucepan, bring the milk and vanilla bean to a boil. Set aside. In a medium bowl, whisk the egg yolks and sugar together until pale in color. Gradually whisk the egg mixture into the vanilla-flavored milk over medium heat and stir until it lightly coats the back of a spoon.

Makes about 2 cups (16 fl oz/500 ml)

Caramel Cages
½ cup (4 fl oz/125 ml) water
1 cup (8 oz/250 g) sugar

In a medium, heavy saucepan, combine the water and sugar and cook over medium heat until golden. Immediately remove from heat and let cool until the caramel begins to harden, about 1 minute.

Using the back of an oiled soup ladle as a mold, make a trellis by dipping a spoon into the caramel and pulling the thread back and forth over the ladle to form a cage. Carefully twist the cage free and place it on a tray. Repeat the process, reheating the caramel in the saucepan as necessary, to form 4 caramel cages.

Makes 4 cages

The Old Rectory
Wicklow, County Wicklow

Built in 1875, this charming Victorian rectory has the architecture and interior detailing typical of all Irish country rectories, down to the marble fireplaces, which are white in the lounge and black in the dining room; a customary way of indicating which room was for wedding parties and which for funerals.

Today the Old Rectory is an elegant small hotel owned and personally managed by Linda and Paul Saunders. It is noted for its tranquil setting, pretty floral decor, romantic guest bedrooms, and Linda's delicious dinners. Visitors use the hotel as a comfortable home base for day trips to Glendalough, Powerscourt Gardens, Wicklow Mountains National Park, or the County Wicklow Gardens Festival in May and June.

As for meals, in the morning guests can choose an Irish, Swiss, or Scottish breakfast to start their day, and in the evening, after aperitifs by a log fire, they are treated to Linda's wholesome cooking, which emphasizes local seafood, meats from a prizewinning butcher, organically grown vegetables, and stunning homemade desserts. The dishes, many of which are vegetarian, are often decorated with edible flowers and fragrant herbs. During the Wicklow Gardens Festival, Linda creates ten-course floral tasting menus. She says, "Eating flowers isn't as unusual as it first seems. It's just an old habit we have mostly forgotten. In Elizabethan times they were regarded as part and parcel of mixed sallets (salads)." The following recipes, created by Linda Saunders, are garnished and flavored with chive flowers, borage blossoms, rosemary flowers, and candied violets.

The Menu
The Old Rectory

Smoked Salmon Parcels Tied with Chives

Fresh Asparagus in Herb Flower Crepes

Light Prawn Soup

Smoked-Pheasant Roulade with Rosemary Cream Sauce

Cheesecake with Raspberry Coulis

Serves Six

Smoked Salmon Parcels Tied with Chives

This pretty hors d'oeuvre is perfect for festive occasions.

4 ounces (125 g) thinly sliced smoked salmon
2 tablespoons cream cheese
½ teaspoon fresh lemon juice
Pinch of freshly ground black pepper
6 fresh chives
1 chive blossom for garnish (optional)

Cut the smoked salmon slices into twelve 1-by-4-inch (2.5-by-10-cm) strips. Finely chop all the trimmings. In a medium bowl, blend the cream cheese, salmon trimmings, lemon juice, and pepper.

Put ½ teaspoon of the cream cheese mixture at the end of each strip of smoked salmon and roll up. Soften the chives by dipping them in boiling water. Pull the chives apart so they split in half lengthwise. Use the strips like string to tie the salmon rolls into parcels, tying the chives into a bow. Complete the presentation by snipping little florets off the chive blossom and slipping the stalk under the bow.

Makes 12 parcels; serves 6

Fresh Asparagus in Herb Flower Crepes

This dish makes a wonderfully light first course that is suitable for vegetarians. Blue borage flowers, which taste a bit like cucumber, may be used in salads and chilled soups, or even be sugared for dessert garnishes. Chive flowers, fennel fronds, dill flowers, and parsley may also be used for this recipe.

Crepe Batter

⅓ cup (2 oz/60 g) unbleached all-purpose flour

½ cup (4 fl oz/125 ml) milk

1 egg

½ teaspoon salt

Vegetable oil for cooking

24 borage flowers, plus more for garnish

Fresh sweet cicely leaves

24 asparagus spears

Melted butter for serving

To make the crepe batter: Put the flour in a medium bowl and whisk in the milk in a thin stream until perfectly smooth. Whisk in the egg and salt. Allow the batter to stand for 3 hours before cooking. (This quantity will make about 8 thin crepes.)

To cook the crepes: Preheat the oven to warm. Heat a crepe pan over medium-high heat until very hot, or until drops of water dance on it. Film the pan with oil, pour 2 tablespoons batter into the center of the pan, and tilt it in all directions. Immediately press 2 borage flowers and some pieces of sweet cicely face up near one edge of the batter, making a nice arrangement. When the first side is lightly browned, after about 50 seconds, shake the pan to dislodge the crepe, then turn it over with your fingers or a spatula and cook on the other side for 15 seconds. Do not overcook. Stack the crepes on a plate, interleaved with parchment or waxed paper, and cover with aluminum foil. Keep warm in the preheated oven.

The Old Rectory

In a pot of salted boiling water, cook the asparagus spears for 5 minutes, or until tender; drain, run under cold water to stop the cooking process, and drain again.

Put 1 crepe flower-side down onto each of 6 warmed plates, place 4 asparagus spears across the center, and fold the crepe over the top, revealing the pressed flowers. Serve with a little melted butter and decorate with borage flowers.

Makes 6 servings

The Old Rectory

Light Prawn Soup

Dillisk, a purplish seaweed found along the coast of Ireland, adds the flavor of the sea to this simple soup; it is usually available dried in natural foods stores.

1 pound (500 g) peeled cooked prawns
5 cups (40 fl oz/1.25 l) fish stock (see page 217)
1 tablespoon finely shredded dried dillisk
1 small onion, finely chopped
1 tablespoon cornstarch
2 tablespoons water
Salt and freshly ground black pepper to taste
Minced fresh herbs for garnish

In a blender or food processor, purée half the prawns with some of the stock.

In a large saucepan, combine the remaining stock, the dillisk, onion, and puréed prawns and bring to a boil. Reduce heat to low and simmer until the onion is soft. In a small bowl, mix the cornstarch with the water; stir this mixture into the soup to thicken it. Season the soup with salt and pepper.

Divide the remaining prawns among 6 soup bowls, ladle in the hot soup, garnish with the herbs, and serve immediately.

Makes 6 servings

Smoked-Pheasant Roulade with Rosemary Cream Sauce

The rings of ingredients in this delicious smoky-flavored roulade make for a fascinating presentation. The roulade is also good served cold.

4 bacon slices
One 3-pound (1.5-kg) smoked pheasant or chicken
Nine 3-inch (7.5-cm) fresh rosemary sprigs
5 cups (40 fl oz/1.25 l) vegetable stock (see page 225) or
   canned vegetable broth
2 pork tenderloins, trimmed
¼ cup (1 ½ oz/45 g) golden raisins
3 tablespoons minced mixed fresh herbs such as parsley,
   chives, and thyme
Salt and freshly ground black pepper to taste
8 ounces (250 g) cream cheese
4 to 6 fresh spinach leaves
Flour seasoned with salt and pepper for coating
Safflower oil for basting
1 tablespoon all-purpose flour
2 tablespoons butter
2 tablespoons heavy (whipping) cream
Rosemary flowers for garnish (optional)
6 fresh rosemary sprigs for garnish

Skin the smoked pheasant or chicken, remove the breasts, and cut off all the other meat. In a large saucepan over high heat, bring the bones and skin, the 9 rosemary sprigs, and the stock or broth to a boil.

In a medium pan of boiling water, cook the bacon for 10 minutes. Drain, rinse, and drain again. Mince all the pheasant and 2 of the bacon slices. Mix in the raisins, minced herbs, salt, and pepper.

Preheat the oven to 400°F (200°C). Lay the trimmed pork tenderloins on a cutting board and, using a sharp knife, cut into the meat as if unrolling a jelly roll. Using a meat pounder, beat into large, thin rectangular scallops. Place 1 of the remaining bacon slices along the longest edge of each and cover it with the minced pheasant mixture. Roll the cream cheese into 2 long sausage shapes the same length as the pork and roll them in the spinach leaves. Make a shallow groove in the minced mixture and place the cream cheese rolls in the grooves. Cover these evenly with the pheasant or chicken breasts. Firmly roll up the pork pieces and secure with kitchen twine. Roll in the seasoned flour. Cover the ends of the roulades with aluminum foil, as they cook the fastest. Baste with the oil.

Bake in the preheated oven for 40 minutes, turning once. Remove from the oven and let sit for 15 minutes before carving.

Strain the stock through a fine-meshed sieve into a medium saucepan; boil to reduce the liquid by half. Transfer to a blender or food processor, add the flour and butter, and blend. Pour into a medium saucepan over high heat and bring to a boil; turn off the heat, then stir in the cream.

Cut each roulade into 12 slices. Pour a little sauce onto each of 6 warm plates and arrange a fan of the pheasant roulade on top. Garnish with optional rosemary flowers and a sprig of rosemary.

Makes 6 servings

Cheesecake with Raspberry Coulis

This cheesecake is best when made the day before it is served so the flavors have a chance to blend.

Crust
14 ounces (440 g) graham crackers or wholemeal biscuits, broken up
¾ cup (6 oz/185 g) butter, melted
½ cup (4 oz/125 g) sugar

Cheese Filling
3 tablespoons butter at room temperature
3 tablespoons sugar
Juice of 1 lemon
12 ounces (375 g) cream cheese at room temperature
¾ cup (6 fl oz/180 ml) heavy (whipping) cream

Raspberry Coulis
1 basket fresh raspberries
Sugar to taste

Garnish
Heavy (whipping) cream
Fresh raspberries

To make the crust: In a blender or food processor, grind the crackers or biscuits to fine crumbs. In a medium bowl, mix the crumbs, butter, and sugar until blended. Press the crumb mixture firmly into an 8½-inch (21.5-cm) springform pan, covering the bottom and reaching nearly halfway up the sides. Refrigerate while making the filling.

To make the filling: In a medium bowl, beat the butter and sugar together until pale and fluffy. Beat in the lemon juice and cream cheese.

The Old Rectory

In a deep bowl, beat the cream until stiff peaks form. Fold the whipped cream into the cream cheese mixture.

Spread the filling evenly over the crumb crust. Cover with plastic wrap and refrigerate for at least 4 hours.

To make the raspberry coulis: In a blender or food processor, purée the raspberries. Strain through a fine-meshed sieve into a bowl and stir in the sugar.

Slice the cheesecake into thin slices and place them on dessert plates. Pour some raspberry coulis around the cheesecake slices. Decorate each plate with dots of cream drawn through into "hearts" and some fresh raspberries.

Makes 6 to 8 servings

Park Hotel Kenmare
Kenmare, County Kerry

The Park Hotel Kenmare was built in 1897 by the Great Southern and Western Railway, and it remained in business as a railway hotel until 1976. After considerable refurbishment, it opened again in the 1980s as an elegant country house hotel.

Today, the Park Hotel offers a gracious retreat from the pressures of modern living and is owned and managed by the friendly and energetic Francis Brennan. The award-winning hotel retains its original Victorian facade, and the interior is especially renowned for luxurious comfort, a relaxed atmosphere, and memorable hospitality. Here, guests may linger with a book or newspaper by crackling wood fires, and stay in bedrooms and suites adorned with works of art, antique furnishings, and marble bathrooms. The spacious grounds include lush gardens, an all-weather tennis court, croquet lawns, and a nine-hole golf course. Sea and lake fishing, horse riding, and many scenic walks are nearby.

According to Francis Brennan, the pride of the hotel is its Michelin star–awarded restaurant. The service, presentation, and innovative menu are as exceptional as the elegant setting. While taking in beautiful views of the estuary, guests dine on marvelous dishes featuring Atlantic salmon, turbot, quail, and succulent Kerry lamb. The cellar contains rare wines (more than five hundred different vintages) and whiskeys and is one of the most highly regarded in Ireland.

THE MENU
Park Hotel Kenmare

Duck Breast Salad with Raspberry Vinaigrette

Cream of Mussel Soup with Brown Soda Bread

Roast Saddle of Lamb with Rosemary-Garlic Sauce

Irish Mist Soufflé

Serves Four

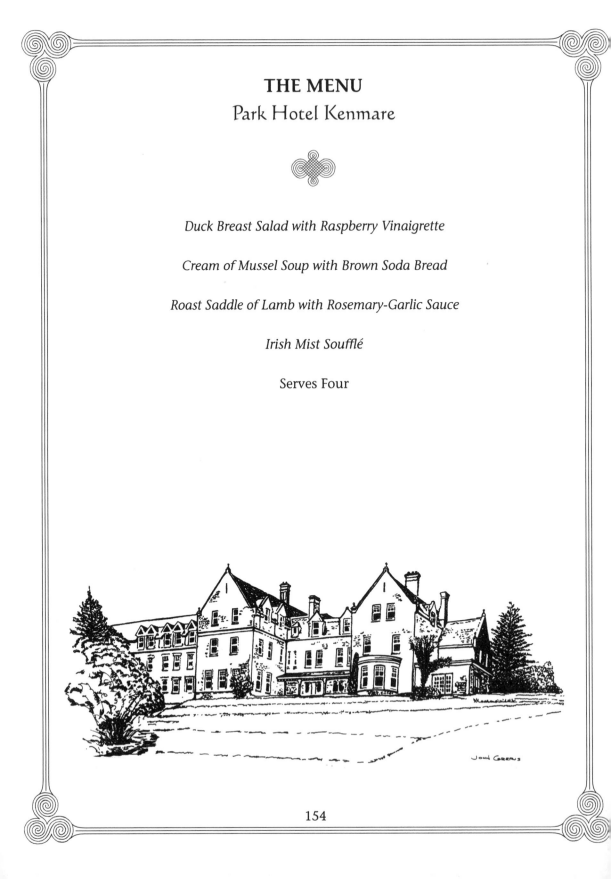

Duck Breast Salad with Raspberry Vinaigrette

Garnish this salad with cherry tomatoes, orange segments, crisp croutons, or raisins marinated in port or madeira if you wish.

Raspberry Vinaigrette
1 basket fresh raspberries
6 tablespoons (3 fl oz/90 ml) olive oil
2 tablespoons white wine vinegar
6 tablespoons (3 fl oz/90 ml) duck stock (see page 216) or
   reduced chicken stock or broth (see page 213)
Salt and freshly ground black pepper to taste

4 handfuls mixed baby greens
2 duck breast halves, trimmed of fat
Salt and freshly ground black pepper to taste
1 tablespoon olive oil

To make the raspberry vinaigrette: In a blender or food processor, purée the raspberries. Add the olive oil, white wine vinegar, and stock or broth. Pass the dressing through a fine-meshed sieve and season with salt and pepper.

Arrange the greens on each of 4 plates.

Slice each duck breast into thin strips and season with salt and pepper. In a large sauté pan or skillet over high heat, heat the oil and cook the ribbons of duck until just slightly pink. Arrange the duck attractively over the lettuce and drizzle with the vinaigrette.

Makes 4 servings

Cream of Mussel Soup with Brown Soda Bread

2 tablespoons olive oil
1 onion, finely chopped
1 celery stalk, chopped
1 leek, white part only, cleaned and finely diced
3 dozen mussels, scrubbed and debearded
1 cup (8 fl oz/250 ml) dry white wine
1 cup (8 fl oz/250 ml) heavy (whipping) cream
Minced fresh parsley to taste
Salt and freshly ground pepper to taste
Brown Soda Bread (recipe follows)

In a large pot over medium-high heat, heat the oil and sauté the onion, celery, and leek until the onion is translucent, about 5 minutes. Add the mussels and white wine, cover, and cook for about 5 minutes, or until the mussels open. Pour the cooking liquid through a fine-meshed strainer into a saucepan. Remove all but 8 mussels from their shells; discard any mussels that have not opened.

Place the saucepan over medium heat, add the cream to the mussel liquid, and bring to a boil. Add the parsley and shucked mussels and season with salt and pepper. Divide the soup among 4 bowls and garnish each bowl with 2 mussels in their shells. Slice the bread and serve with the soup.

Makes 4 servings

Brown Soda Bread

This wholesome quick bread is easy to make at home and goes well with many dishes, including soups, starters, and seafood, and of course it is delicious with sweet butter and homemade preserves or honey. Try to use the bread on the day of baking if possible.

¾ cup (4 oz/125 g) all-purpose flour
½ teaspoon salt
1 teaspoon baking soda
2⅓ cups (12 oz/375 g) whole-wheat flour
2 tablespoons sugar
3 tablespoons wheat germ (optional)
⅓ cup (1 oz/30 g) miller's bran
2 tablespoons cold butter
1 to 1½ cups (8 to 12 fl oz/250 to 375 ml) buttermilk

Preheat the oven to 425°F (220°C). Sift the all-purpose flour, salt, and baking soda together into a large bowl. Sir in the whole-wheat flour, sugar, optional wheat germ, and bran. Using a pastry cutter or your fingers, cut in the butter to make fine crumbs, then add enough buttermilk to make a fairly soft dough.

On a floured board, knead the dough lightly and form into a circle about 1½ inches (3.5 cm) thick. Place on a greased baking sheet, make a deep cross in the top with a floured knife, and bake in the preheated oven for 45 minutes, or until browned and hollow-sounding when tapped on the bottom. Turn the baking sheet around halfway through the baking.

Makes 1 loaf

Roast Saddle of Lamb with Rosemary-Garlic Sauce

One 2-pound (1-kg) boned and rolled saddle of lamb
2 garlic cloves, crushed
Pinch of minced fresh rosemary
1 cup (8 fl oz/250 ml) lamb stock (see page 217), chicken stock
  (see page 213), or canned low-salt chicken broth
Salt and freshly ground black pepper to taste
Homemade potato chips (see page 222) for garnish

Remove the lamb from the refrigerator 30 minutes before cooking. Preheat the oven to 425°F (220°C). In a large skillet over high heat, heat the oil and brown the saddle of lamb on all sides. Transfer the lamb to a roasting pan, reserving the skillet and drippings. Bake the lamb in the preheated oven for 45 minutes, or until a meat thermometer reads 140°F (60°C). Remove from the oven and let sit for 15 minutes before carving.

Heat the drippings in the reserved skillet over medium-low heat. Add the garlic and rosemary and cook for 2 minutes. Add the stock or broth and simmer for 10 minutes to reduce the liquid to ¾ cup (6 fl oz/180 ml). Season with salt and pepper and keep warm.

Cut the lamb into slices. Pool some sauce on each of 4 warm plates and arrange one quarter of the lamb slices on top. Garnish with homemade potato chips.

Makes 4 servings

Irish Mist Soufflé

Irish Mist is a delicious liqueur made from Irish whiskey, honey, and herbs.

2 oranges
1 cup (8 fl oz/250 ml) milk
3 egg yolks
4 tablespoons (2 oz/60 g) sugar
2 tablespoons flour
¼ cup (2 fl oz/60 ml) Irish Mist liqueur
5 egg whites
Powdered sugar for dusting

Prepare a 6-cup (48–fl oz/1.5-l) soufflé dish by buttering it, including the rim, and sprinkling it with granulated sugar. Grate the zest from the oranges. Cut off the bottom and top of the oranges down to the flesh, then cut off the peel. Cut the segments out from between the membranes. Set aside in a colander.

In a small saucepan over low heat, heat the milk until small bubbles form around the edges.

In a medium bowl, beat the egg yolks, orange zest, and 2 tablespoons of the granulated sugar until thick and pale in color. Stir in the flour. Gradually whisk the hot milk into the egg yolk mixture, blend well, and return to the pan over low heat. Whisk until the mixture just comes to a boil, reduce heat to low, and simmer for about 2 minutes, or until thickened enough to coat the back of a spoon. Remove from heat and let cool slightly. Stir in the Irish Mist.

Preheat the oven to 425°F (220°C). In a large bowl, whisk the egg whites until soft peaks form. Gradually beat in the remaining 2 tablespoons granulated sugar until stiff, glossy peaks form.

Heat the liqueur mixture just until hot to the touch. Remove from heat and stir in one-fourth of the egg whites. Fold this mixture into the remaining egg whites as lightly as possible. Spoon the mixture into the

159

soufflé dish. Smooth the surface and quickly arrange the orange segments into a star pattern on top. Bake for 12 to 15 minutes, or until the soufflé is puffed and brown. Dust with powdered sugar and serve at once.

Makes 4 servings

Rathmullan House
Rathmullan, Letterkenny, County Donegal

A superb eighteenth-century Georgian house set in prizewinning gardens on the shores of Lough Swilly, Rathmullan House welcomes guests with a blazing fire in the drawing room and delicious five-course dinners. It is located in the very north of Ireland in the wild and beautiful county of Donegal.

Proprietors Robin and Bob Wheeler completely refurbished Rathmullan in the early 1960s and have run it ever since as a friendly and informal country house hotel celebrating a past era of gentility and good taste. There are twenty-three comfortable bedrooms; three sitting rooms with antique furnishings, oil paintings, and cozy log fires; and fully equipped chalets for families on the grounds. The house itself features intricate plasterwork ceilings, crystal chandeliers, marble fireplaces, and stunning views of the mountains across Lough Swilly. To completely pamper visitors, there is an indoor heated saltwater pool, sauna, and steam room; outdoors, there are sandy beaches, tennis courts, croquet lawns, and many nature walks. Golf, deep-sea fishing, and horse riding are all close by.

Rathmullan is known for its generous, award-winning breakfasts. In the canopied dining room, guests feast on traditionally Irish food: locally caught salmon and sea trout, and Donegal lamb and beef. Chef Kevin Murphy, who changes his imaginative dinner menu daily, offers here some of his most popular recipes.

The Menu
Rathmullan House

Guinea Hen and Herb Terrine with Wild Mushrooms

Seafood Soup

Chicken and Mushrooms in Puff Pastry with Tomato-Tarragon Sauce

Marie's Bakewell Tart

Serves Eight

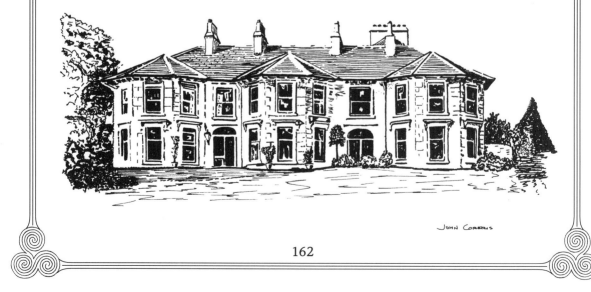

JOHN CORBUS

Guinea Hen and Herb Terrine with Wild Mushrooms

Refrigerate this terrine for a day or two before serving to allow it to develop its full flavor.

1 pound (500 g) guinea hen breasts, boned, skinned, and chopped
Salt and freshly ground black pepper to taste
2 teaspoons minced mixed fresh herbs such as rosemary, thyme,
  and marjoram
8 bacon slices
½ cup (2 oz/60 g) julienned carrots
½ cup (2 oz/60 g) finely diced carrots
½ cup (2 oz/60 g) julienned zucchini
1 teaspoon olive oil
2 ounces (60 g) wild mushrooms, chopped
⅔ cup (5 fl oz/160 ml) heavy (whipping) cream
Cumberland Sauce (see page 214) or cranberry jelly for serving

Finely dice enough guinea hen meat to make 2 tablespoonfuls. Set aside. In a blender or food processor, purée the remaining guinea hen meat with the salt, pepper, and herbs until fairly smooth. Cover and refrigerate.

In a medium pan of boiling water, cook the bacon for 10 minutes. Drain, rinse, and drain again. Line a 6-cup (48–fl oz/1.5-l) loaf terrine mold with plastic wrap and then the bacon, letting the bacon extend over the rim. In a pot of salted boiling water, separately blanch the julienned carrots, diced carrots, and zucchini for 2 minutes each; drain and rinse each under cold water.

Preheat the oven to 350°F (180°C). In a sauté pan or skillet over medium heat, heat the olive oil and sauté the mushrooms and the reserved diced guinea hen meat. Return the refrigerated guinea hen purée to the blender or food processor and, on high speed, gradually add the cream until blended.

Divide the purée equally between 2 bowls. Add the diced carrots and the mushroom mixture to one bowl; stir until well blended.

Rathmullan House

Using 2 piping bags, pipe alternate layers of the 2 purées, with the julienned carrots and zucchini in between. Fold the bacon ends and then the plastic wrap over the terrine and cover with a double layer of aluminum foil.

Place the terrine in a baking pan and fill the pan with warm water to halfway up the sides of the terrine. Bake in the preheated oven for 1 hour and 15 minutes. Let cool for 1 hour, then refrigerate overnight. Just before serving, set the terrine in a pan of hot water for a few seconds to loosen, pour out any fat and juices, and invert onto a platter. Slice thinly and serve with Cumberland sauce or cranberry jelly.

Makes 8 servings

Seafood Soup

Use a combination of whatever fish and shellfish is freshest and best. This soup can be a meal in itself served with brown soda bread (see page 157) and butter.

2 tablespoons butter

2½ cups (12 oz/375 g) finely chopped mixed vegetables
   (onions, carrots, celery, leek)

1 teaspoon chopped fennel

2 tablespoons Cognac or brandy

⅔ cup (4 oz/125 g) chopped tomato

1 teaspoon tomato purée

⅓ cup (2 oz/60 g) flour

4 cups (32 fl oz/1 l) fish stock (see page 217), heated

1 pound (500 g) cooked fish and/or shellfish, such as cod,
   haddock, mussels, scallops, and prawns

1 cup (8 fl oz/250 ml) heavy (whipping) cream

Salt and cracked black pepper to taste

In a large sauté pan or skillet, melt the butter over medium heat and sauté the chopped vegetables and fennel until the onion is translucent, about 7 minutes. Raise heat to high, stir in the Cognac or brandy, and cook to reduce the liquid. Stir in the tomatoes, tomato purée, flour, and stock, stirring constantly. Bring to a boil, then reduce heat to low and simmer for 30 minutes. Add the fish and simmer for 5 minutes. Remove from heat and stir in the cream, salt, and pepper. Serve immediately.

Makes 8 servings

Rathmullan House

Chicken and Mushrooms in Puff Pastry
with Tomato-Tarragon Sauce

A wonderful dish for a special dinner party.

1 tablespoon butter
2 pounds (1 kg) mushrooms, chopped
1½ pounds (750 g) boneless, skinless chicken, chopped
Salt and freshly ground black pepper to taste
1 bunch fresh spinach, stemmed
8 boneless, skinless chicken breast halves
⅔ cup (5 fl oz/160 ml) heavy (whipping) cream
2 pounds (1 kg) puff pastry, cut into ten 2½-by-5-inch
   (6-by-13-cm) rectangles
Tomato-Tarragon Sauce (recipe follows)

In a large sauté pan or skillet, melt the butter over medium-high heat and sauté the mushrooms for 5 minutes, or until all the moisture has evaporated. Transfer the mushrooms to a bowl, cover, and refrigerate for at least 1 hour.

In a blender or food processor, purée the chopped chicken with the salt and pepper. Transfer to a bowl, cover, and refrigerate for at least 1 hour.

In a pot of salted boiling water, blanch the spinach for 2 minutes; drain and lay flat on paper towels.

Preheat the oven to 400°F (200°C). Meanwhile, using a meat pounder, flatten the chicken breasts to a ¼-inch (6-mm) thickness. Season the chicken with salt and pepper and cover with a layer of blanched spinach.

Return the chicken mixture to the blender or food processor and, with the motor running, gradually pour in the cream. Fold in the mushrooms.

Spread a layer of the chicken mixture on top of the spinach and roll up each chicken breast. Wrap each chicken roll in a piece of puff pastry. Place the rolls on a greased baking sheet, seam-side down, and bake in the

Rathmullan House

preheated oven for 15 to 20 minutes, or until the puff pastry is golden brown. Let sit before slicing. Serve with tomato-tarragon sauce.

Makes 8 servings

Tomato-Tarragon Sauce
2 tablespoons unsalted butter
4 shallots, minced
½ garlic clove, crushed
1 teaspoon minced fresh tarragon
4 tomatoes, chopped
½ cup (4 fl oz/125 ml) dry white wine
2 cups (16 fl oz/500 ml) chicken stock (see page 213) or
  canned low-salt chicken broth
Salt and freshly ground black pepper to taste

In a medium sauté pan or skillet, melt the butter over medium heat. Sauté the shallots and garlic for 5 minutes. Add the tarragon and chopped tomatoes and cook until dry. Stir in the wine and stock or broth and cook to reduce the liquid to ¾ cup (6 fl oz/180 ml). Season with salt and pepper.

Makes about 1½ cups (12 fl oz/375 ml)

Marie's Bakewell Tart

An easy-to-make treat with a layer of raspberry jam topped with a rich almond paste filling. This luscious version of the classic Bakewell tart is a standout dessert.

Crust
1⅓ cups (7 oz/220 g) unbleached all-purpose flour
¼ cup (2 oz/60 g) sugar
¼ teaspoon salt
½ cup (4 oz/125 g) cold unsalted butter, cut into pieces
¼ cup (2 fl oz/60 ml) ice water

Filling
½ cup (4 oz/125 g) unsalted butter at room temperature
⅔ cup (5 oz/155 g) sugar
1¼ cups (6 oz/185 g) almonds, ground
2 tablespoons all-purpose flour
3 large eggs, beaten
1 tablespoon Amaretto or almond extract
5 tablespoons (3 oz/90 g) raspberry jam
Sliced almonds for decoration

To make the crust: In a medium bowl, combine the flour, sugar, and salt. Cut the butter into the flour mixture using a pastry cutter or 2 knives until the mixture is the texture of coarse meal. Sprinkle in the water and mix with a fork until the mixture forms a mass. Or, process the butter, flour, sugar, and salt in a blender or food processor until the mixture resembles coarse meal. Add the water and process until the dough forms a mass.

Press the dough into a flat disk, wrap in plastic wrap, and refrigerate for at least 30 minutes. Roll out the dough between sheets of waxed paper to a ⅛-inch (3-mm) thickness. Transfer the dough to a 9-inch-diameter (23-cm) tart pan with a removable bottom; trim the edges and refrigerate for 30 minutes.

To make the filling: In a large bowl, beat the butter and sugar together until light and fluffy. In another large bowl, mix the ground almonds and flour. Alternately stir the eggs and the almond mixture by halves into the butter mixture, beating well after each addition. Stir in the liqueur or extract.

Preheat the oven to 350°F (180°C). Spread the raspberry jam over the bottom of the crust. Spread the filling evenly over the jam. Decorate the tart with sliced almonds. Bake in the preheated oven for 40 minutes, or until the filling is set and top is golden. Let cool to room temperature before slicing and serving.

Makes one 9-inch (23-cm) tart

Rathsallagh House
Dunlavin, County Wicklow

Converted from Queen Anne stables in 1798, Rathsallagh is a large, comfortable country house situated amid five hundred acres of spacious lawns, peaceful woods, and rolling farmland. Presided over by Kay and Joe O'Flynn, who cheerfully encourage their guests to drop all cares and enjoy themselves, Rathsallagh offers seventeen rooms and a happy, relaxed atmosphere.

Rathsallagh's own grounds are a sportsman's paradise and provide opportunities for horse riding, hunting, pony trekking, archery, clay pigeon shooting, and tennis in the beautiful walled garden. Many visitors enjoy spending their time on the estate's magnificent eighteen-hole championship golf course or visiting Glendalough, Kilkenny, or the Curragh, Naas, or Punchestown racecourses. When it rains, guests can sit before log fires reading or playing board games, make use of the indoor swimming pool and billiards room, or head off to the theaters and museums of nearby Dublin.

Winner of the country house Breakfast of the Year award in 1988, 1990, and 1994, Rathsallagh's breakfast is served Edwardian style from silver chafing dishes on the sideboard. The buffet includes fresh orange juice, rhubarb compote, natural yogurt, Irish farmhouse cheeses, eggs, ham, smoked salmon, field mushrooms, bacon, homemade sausages, traditional black and white puddings, pastries, and homemade breads. An equally bountiful afternoon tea is provided later in the drawing room or garden. The elegant dining room features the best from Rathsallagh's own kitchen gardens and local growers, fish from Wexford and Youghal boats, game in season, Nolan's lamb, and McPartland's beef. To complete the meal, a spectacular dessert trolley with a huge carved ice bowl full of homemade ice cream, and a selection of cakes, tarts, tortes, meringues, fruits, cream, and Irish farmhouse cheeses is wheeled around the dining room. All food is prepared under the supervision of Kay O'Flynn, who created the following Christmas menu.

THE MENU
Rathsallagh House
A Christmas Menu

Grilled Oysters with Beurre Blanc

Cream of Wild Mushroom Soup

Roast Pheasant with Apples and Bread Sauce

Almond Baskets with Brown-Bread Ice Cream and Berries

Serves Four

John Corbis

Grilled Oysters with Beurre Blanc

Serve with brown soda bread and sweet butter (see page 157). For festive occasions, garnish each oyster with 1 teaspoon of caviar.

Beurre Blanc
½ teaspoon minced shallot
1 bay leaf
1½tablespoons wine vinegar
1½ tablespoons water
½ cup (4 oz/125 g) chilled unsalted butter, cut into 8 pieces
1 tablespoon heavy (whipping) cream
Salt and ground white pepper to taste
6 black peppercorns
Squeeze of fresh lemon juice

12 Galway Bay or other large oysters in the shell
Lemon wedges for serving

To make the beurre blanc: In a small saucepan, combine the shallot, bay leaf, vinegar, and water and cook over medium-high heat to reduce the liquid to 2 tablespoons. Whisk in the butter piece by piece; be careful not to let the mixture boil. Stir in the cream, salt, pepper, peppercorns, and lemon juice. Strain through a fine-meshed sieve and discard the bay leaf and peppercorns.

Preheat the broiler. Shuck the oysters and return each to its deeper half shell. Arrange the oysters on the broiling pan and pour a little buerre blanc over them. Broil under the preheated broiler for about 3 minutes, or until the edges curl. Serve immediately with lemon wedges.

Makes 4 servings

Cream of Wild Mushroom Soup

Wild mushrooms have been eaten in Ireland for centuries, and many different varieties grow there abundantly. There is also a large cultivated-mushroom industry in Ireland, and these are in season year-round.

2 tablespoons butter
2 shallots, minced
1 garlic clove, minced
4 ounces (125 g) shiitake mushrooms, stemmed and chopped
4 ounces (125 g) oyster mushrooms, chopped
4 ounces (125 g) crimini or field mushrooms, chopped
¼ cup (⅓ oz/10 g) minced fresh parsley
4 bread slices, crusts removed, torn into pieces
3 cups (24 fl oz/750 ml) chicken stock (see page 213) or
    canned low-salt chicken broth
Salt and freshly ground black pepper to taste
1 bay leaf
Pinch of ground nutmeg
1 cup (8 fl oz/250 ml) heavy (whipping) cream

In a large saucepan, melt the butter over medium heat and sauté the shallots until tender, about 4 minutes. Stir in the garlic, mushrooms, and half the parsley. Reduce heat to low, cover, and cook for 3 minutes. Stir in the bread, stock or broth, salt, pepper, bay leaf, and nutmeg. Raise heat to high and bring to a boil. Reduce heat and simmer for 10 minutes. Remove the bay leaf.

Transfer the mixture to a blender or food processor and purée. Return the soup to the saucepan and place over medium-low heat. Stir in the cream, remaining parsley, salt, and pepper to taste. Heat for 2 minutes, then serve.

Makes 4 to 6 servings

Rathsallagh House

Roast Pheasant with Apples and Bread Sauce

Pheasant is lean, with the largest breast of all the game birds. If it is unavailable, two Cornish game hens may be substituted for each pheasant. Bread sauce is also traditionally served with roast turkey and chicken.

4 tablespoons (2 oz/60 g) butter at room temperature

1 onion, chopped

2 large tart apples, peeled and chopped

6 juniper berries, crushed

Salt and freshly ground pepper to taste

2 pheasants

6 bacon slices

1 cup (8 fl oz/250 ml) pheasant stock (see page 221) or
   reduced chicken stock or broth (see page 213)

Buttered Crumbs

½ cup (4 oz/125 g) butter

¾ cup (1½ oz/45 g) fresh bread crumbs made from day-old bread

Bread Sauce

6 whole cloves

1 large onion

1 cup (8 fl oz/250 ml) milk

1 cup (2 oz/60 g) fresh white bread crumbs

Salt and ground white pepper to taste

4 tablespoons (2 oz/60 g) butter

2 tablespoons heavy (whipping) cream

⅔ cup (5 fl oz/160 ml) dry red wine

2 fresh thyme sprigs

2 fresh parsley sprigs

1 piece dried orange peel

Watercress for garnish

In a large sauté pan or skillet, melt 2 tablespoons of the butter over medium heat and sauté the onion for 5 minutes. Add the apples and sauté for 5 minutes, or until tender. Remove from heat and stir in the juniper berries, salt, and pepper.

Rinse the pheasants thoroughly and dry completely. Reserve the giblets, except the liver. Preheat the oven to 375°F (190°C). Season the pheasants inside and out with salt and pepper. Place the onion mixture inside the cavity. Spread the remaining 2 tablespoons butter over the pheasant and cover the breasts with the bacon. Place the pheasants on their sides in a roasting pan.

Bake in the preheated oven for 15 minutes, then turn, baste with the pan drippings, and bake 15 minutes more. Turn the pheasants breast-side up and baste again. Bake another 20 minutes, or until the juices run clear when the inside of the thighs are pierced. Remove the bacon for the last 10 minutes of the cooking time.

Meanwhile, combine the giblets and game stock in a small saucepan. Bring to a boil, reduce heat, and simmer for about 20 minutes. Strain.

To make the buttered crumbs: Melt the butter in a large sauté pan or skillet over low heat. Add the crumbs and cook, stirring, until the crumbs are browned and crisp. Using a slotted spoon, transfer to paper towels to drain, then transfer to a warm serving bowl and keep warm.

To make the bread sauce: Stick the cloves in the onion. Place in a medium saucepan and add the milk. Bring slowly to a boil, reduce heat to low, and simmer until ready to serve. Remove the onion. Add the remaining ingredients. Pour into a warm sauceboat.

When the pheasants are cooked, transfer them to a warm serving dish and let sit for 15 minutes. Add the wine to the roasting pan, bring to a boil, and stir to scrape up the browned bits from the bottom of the pan. Add the stock, thyme, parsley, and orange peel, reduce heat, and simmer for a few minutes. Remove the orange peel and continue simmering until reduced by half. Pour into a warm gravy boat.

Decorate the pheasants with watercress and a sprinkling of crumbs and serve with the remaining crumbs, pan sauce, and bread sauce.

Makes 4 servings

Rathsallagh House

Almond Baskets with Brown-Bread Ice Cream and Berries

In this pretty dessert, tuiles are formed into cups and filled with ice cream, then served garnished with puréed and whole berries.

Almond Baskets

2 egg whites

½ cup (4 oz/125 g) sugar

⅓ cup (2 oz/60 g) all-purpose flour

½ teaspoon vanilla extract

¼ cup (1 oz/30 g) sliced blanched almonds

4 tablespoons (2 oz/60 g) butter, melted

Brown-Bread Ice Cream (recipe follows)

1 cup (4 oz/125 g) fresh strawberries or raspberries
  or a mixture of both

Sugar to taste

Dash of kirsch (optional)

Fresh mint sprigs for garnish

To make the baskets: Preheat the oven to 350°F (180°C). Lightly oil 2 baking sheets and the outsides of 4 drinking glasses.

In a large bowl, beat the egg whites and sugar until foamy. Sift in the flour and add the vanilla, almonds, and butter; stir until well blended.

Place 3 to 4 teaspoonfuls of the mixture at least 5 inches apart on a baking sheet and flatten with the bottom of a glass. Cook about 3 or 4 cookies at a time. Bake in the preheated oven until browned at the edges but pale in the middle, about 5 or 6 minutes. Remove from the oven and let cool a few seconds. Lift carefully with a metal spatula and, while warm and pliable, place each on an upturned glass and form gently into a pleated basket shape. Let cool completely on a wire tray. Continue until all of the batter is used.

Rathsallagh House

To serve, purée half of the strawberries or raspberries, or a mixture, with a little sugar and a dash of kirsch if desired. Place a spoonful of purée to one side of each dessert plate. Place an almond basket on the other. Put a scoop of ice cream in each basket. Decorate with a sprig of mint and some whole berries on top of the purée.

Makes 4 servings

Brown-Bread Ice Cream

1½ cups (3 oz/90 g) fresh coarse brown bread crumbs (see page 157)
2 tablespoons packed brown sugar
6 eggs, separated
¾ cup (6 oz/185 g) sugar
2 cups (16 fl oz/500 ml) heavy (whipping) cream

Preheat the oven to 375°F (190°C). In a medium bowl, mix the crumbs and brown sugar together and spread out on a baking sheet. Bake in the preheated oven, stirring occasionally, until crisp and golden brown, about 15 minutes. Let cool completely, then crush coarsely with a rolling pin.

In a medium bowl, beat the egg whites until soft peaks form, then beat in the sugar, 1 tablespoon at a time, and continue beating until the mixture forms stiff, glossy peaks. In a deep bowl, beat the cream until soft peaks form. In a medium bowl, beat the egg yolks until pale in color. Fold the cream, egg yolks, and crumbs into the egg-white mixture. Freeze in an ice cream maker according to the manufacturer's instructions.

Makes about 6 cups

Rathsallagh House

Rosleague Manor
Letterfrack, County Galway

If you enjoy relaxing stays in period houses, you couldn't do better than to visit Rosleague, an 1820s Regency manor house with a superb view of Ballinakill Bay in the west of Ireland. It has been owned and personally managed since 1971 by the sister-and-brother team of Anne and Patrick Foyle, who have furnished the house with well-chosen antiques and gracefully converted it into a first-class hotel of infinite charm.

Anne and Patrick welcome all guests with heartfelt warmth and oversee every detail. Rosleague's many amenities include peat fires, a billiards room, two delightful drawing rooms, a sauna, an all-weather tennis court, and a recently added Victorian-style conservatory. A short walk through a secluded garden takes you to the ocean's edge, and beautiful beaches are within easy reach. In addition, golf, horse riding, cycling, and salmon and trout fishing are all available, and Rosleague is next to Connemara's new five-thousand-acre national park.

Rosleague's elegant dining room is hung with oil paintings and candle-lit for dinner. Head chef Nigel Rush offers superb cuisine with a special focus on Connemara lamb, freshly caught seafood from Cleggan harbor, Irish farmhouse cheeses, and home-grown vegetables and herbs.

THE MENU
Rosleague Manor

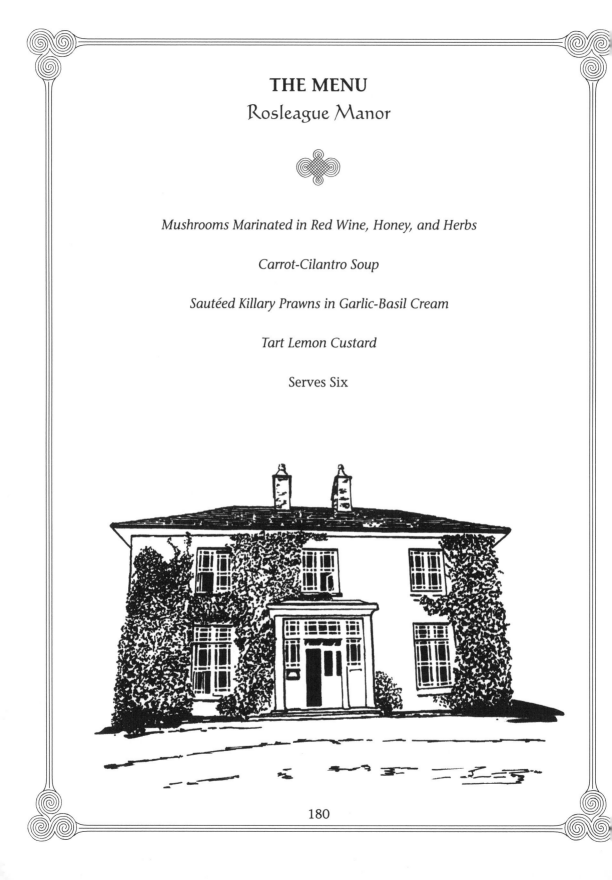

Mushrooms Marinated in Red Wine, Honey, and Herbs

Carrot-Cilantro Soup

Sautéed Killary Prawns in Garlic-Basil Cream

Tart Lemon Custard

Serves Six

Mushrooms Marinated in Red Wine, Honey, and Herbs

Prepare this recipe the day before you plan to serve it.

⅓ cup (3 fl oz/80 ml) fresh tomato purée
2 tablespoons honey
4 garlic cloves, crushed
⅓ cup (3 fl oz/80 ml) vegetable oil
Pinch of minced fresh herbs such as parley, chives,
  watercress, thyme, marjoram
2 bay leaves
½ cup (4 fl oz/125 ml) dry red wine
2 pounds (1 kg) fresh button mushrooms

In a large saucepan, combine the tomato purée, honey, garlic, oil, herbs, bay leaves, and red wine and bring to a simmer over medium heat. Stir in the mushrooms and simmer for 30 minutes. Remove from heat and refrigerate overnight. Just before serving, reheat.

Makes 6 servings

Carrot-Cilantro Soup

3 carrots, peeled and chopped

½ cup (2½ oz/75 g) chopped celery

½ cup (2 oz/60 g) chopped onion

1 potato, peeled and chopped

1 handful fresh cilantro (fresh coriander) leaves

4 cups (32 fl oz/1 l) chicken stock (see page 213) or
   canned low-salt chicken broth

½ cup (4 fl oz/125 ml) heavy (whipping) cream, or to taste

In a large saucepan, combine the carrots, celery, onion, potato, and cilantro leaves; pour in the stock or broth and bring to a boil over medium heat. Reduce heat to low and simmer for 30 minutes. Transfer to a blender or food processor and purée. Return to the saucepan over medium heat. Stir in the cream, cook for 2 minutes, and serve.

Makes 6 servings

Sautéed Killary Prawns in Garlic-Basil Cream

2 tablespoons clarified butter (see page 214)
2¼ pounds (1.1 kg) Killary prawns or other large
   prawns, peeled and deveined
3 garlic cloves, crushed
12 fresh basil leaves
1½ cups (12 fl oz/375 ml) heavy (whipping) cream

In a large sauté pan or skillet over medium heat, heat enough clarified butter to coat the bottom of the pan. Sauté the prawns until pink and opaque, about 3 to 4 minutes. Stir in the remaining ingredients and cook to reduce the liquid until it lightly coats the back of a spoon. Serve immediately.

Makes 6 servings

Tart Lemon Custard

⅔ cup (5 oz/160 ml) heavy (whipping) cream
5 eggs
1 cup (8 oz/250 g) sugar
Juice of 2 lemons

Preheat the oven to 250°F (120°C). In a deep bowl, beat the cream until soft peaks form. In a medium bowl, beat the eggs and sugar together until pale in color. Stir in the lemon juice and gently fold in the whipped cream. Pour into 6 individual ramekins. Place the ramekins in a baking pan and add warm water to halfway up the sides of the ramekins. Bake in the preheated oven for 30 minutes. Let cool. Refrigerate for 3 to 4 hours, or until ready to serve.

Makes 6 servings

Sheen Falls Lodge
Kenmare, County Kerry

Situated in the picturesque town of Kenmare in the southwest of Ireland, the Sheen Falls estate dates back to the 1700s. After an extensive refurbishment and expansion during the 1980s, the manor house opened as a luxury hotel in 1991. Sheen Falls Lodge has been garnering international acclaim ever since and is a member of Relais & Chateaux.

Typifying elegance in a country setting, the lodge carries on country house traditions on a wooded three-hundred-acre estate above the Sheen Waterfalls and Kenmare Bay. Guests can try their hand at salmon and trout fishing along the Sheen River, horse riding, clay-target shooting, tennis, jogging, or golfing on the Kenmare eighteen-hole course. Indoor pursuits include health and beauty treatments at the fitness center, games in the billiards room, and relaxing in a leather armchair with a book from the fifteen-hundred-volume library.

The following recipes were created by head chef Fergus Moore, who has worked at some of the top hotels and restaurants in Holland, Germany, Australia, and Ireland. His cooking has been awarded a prestigious Michelin star at La Cascade restaurant, where his sophisticated menu features the finest regional produce, game in season, fresh seafood, and home-smoked wild salmon. Wines from the cellar complement the menu, and there is a nightly performance of piano music in the restaurant.

THE MENU
Sheen Falls Lodge

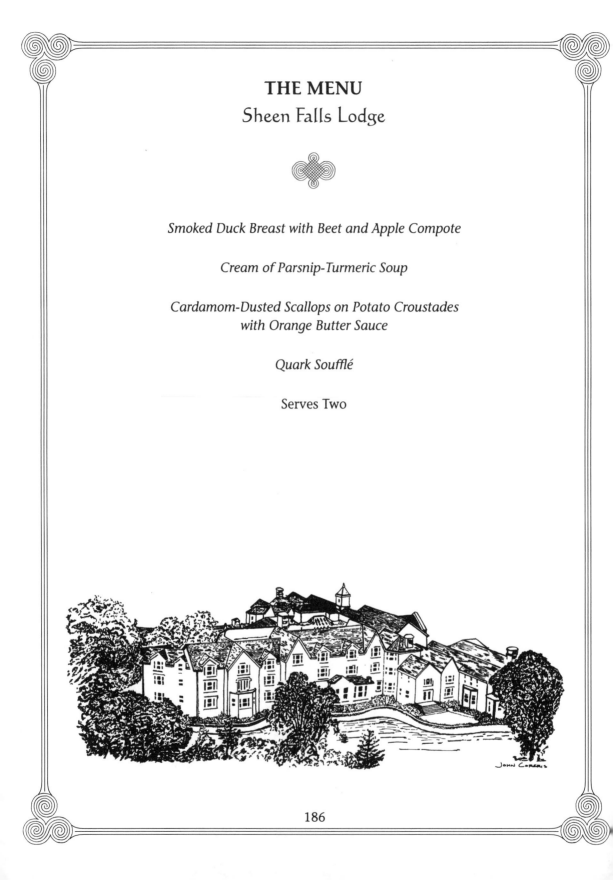

Smoked Duck Breast with Beet and Apple Compote

Cream of Parsnip-Turmeric Soup

*Cardamom-Dusted Scallops on Potato Croustades
with Orange Butter Sauce*

Quark Soufflé

Serves Two

Smoked Duck Breast with Beet and Apple Compote

Serve with a little butter sauce (see page 213) drizzled around the compote if you like.

1 large beet
1 handful apple wood chips
1 duck breast half, skinned and boned
1 tablespoon butter
6 shallots, diced
2 tablespoons crème de cassis
2 tablespoons grenadine
½ teaspoon raspberry vinegar
½ teaspoon sugar
1 apple, peeled, cored, and diced
Arrowroot for thickening, if necessary
Warmed honey for brushing
Butter Sauce (see page 213), optional

Cook the beet in salted boiling water to cover until tender, about 30 minutes to 1 hour. Using a slotted spoon, transfer to a colander to cool; reserve the cooking liquid. Peel and finely dice the beet. Set aside.

Prepare a smoker or a low charcoal fire in a grill. Soak the wood chips in water to cover for 30 minutes. Drain the chips and sprinkle them in a roasting pan. Place the duck breast on a wire rack over the roasting pan. Smoke in the smoker or the covered grill for 3 to 5 minutes. Set aside.

Preheat the oven to 350°F (180°C). In a large sauté pan or skillet, melt the butter over medium heat and sauté the shallots for 3 minutes. Add the beet, crème de cassis, grenadine, vinegar, sugar, and reserved beet cooking liquid to taste. Taste and adjust the seasoning. Add the diced apple and cook for 3 to 5 minutes to reduce the sauce; thicken with a little arrowroot if necessary.

Brush the duck breast with a little honey and bake in the preheated oven for 30 minutes, or until browned outside but pink inside. Remove from the oven and let sit for 10 to 15 minutes. Place the beet and apple compote on each of 2 plates. Thinly slice the duck, arrange the slices on top of the compote, and serve with butter sauce, if you like.

Makes 2 servings

Cream of Parsnip-Turmeric Soup

1 tablespoon butter
5 small parsnips, peeled and finely diced
1 leek (white part only), cleaned and finely diced
½ celery stalk, finely diced
1 onion, finely diced
½ fennel bulb, trimmed, cored, and finely diced
1 apple, peeled, cored, and finely diced
1 garlic clove, minced
2 tablespoons ground turmeric
4 cups (32 fl oz/1 l) chicken stock (see page 213) or
   canned low-salt chicken broth
Salt and freshly ground black pepper to taste
⅓ cup (3 fl oz/90 ml) heavy (whipping) cream

In a large saucepan, melt the butter over medium-low heat and sauté the parsnips, leek, celery, onion, fennel, apple, and garlic for about 7 minutes, or until tender. Stir in the turmeric, raise heat to medium, and sauté for 2 to 3 minutes. Stir in the stock or broth and simmer for 5 minutes. Transfer to a blender or food processor and purée. Strain through a fine-meshed sieve into a clean saucepan. Add the salt, pepper, and cream. Heat over medium-low heat for 3 to 5 minutes and serve.

Makes 4 servings

Cardamom-Dusted Scallops on Potato Croustades with Orange Butter Sauce

1⅓ cups (11 fl oz/330 ml) fresh orange juice
6 star anise pods
4 potatoes, peeled
Salt and freshly ground black pepper to taste
¼ cup (2 oz/60 g) clarified butter (see page 214)
6 tablespoons (3 fl oz/90 ml) heavy (whipping) cream
½ cup (4 oz/125 g) unsalted butter, cut into pieces
12 sea scallops
Freshly ground cardamom for dusting
1 tablespoon olive oil
15 chives, minced

In a small, heavy saucepan, combine the orange juice and star anise. Cook over medium-low heat until reduced to ½ cup (4 fl oz/125 ml), keeping the sides of the saucepan clean by brushing them with a wet brush so the orange juice does not color.

Meanwhile, shred the potatoes and season with salt and pepper. In a large sauté pan or skillet over medium heat, heat the clarified butter, spoon in 6 heaping tablespoons of the shredded potatoes, and flatten them into 6 thin patties. Fry the patties until crisp, about 4 minutes on each side. Set aside and keep warm.

Add the cream to the reduced orange juice mixture and bring to a boil. Remove from heat and whisk in the butter until incorporated. Season with salt and pepper to taste and strain through a fine-meshed sieve. Set aside and keep warm.

Season the scallops with salt and pepper and dust with cardamom. In a large sauté pan or skillet over high heat, heat the olive oil and fry the scallops until opaque in the center and lightly browned, about 3 minutes.

Place a potato croustade on each of 2 plates and arrange 3 scallops on top, follow with another croustade, 3 more scallops, and finally the last croustade. Add the chives to the sauce and pour the sauce around. Serve immediately.

Makes 2 servings

Sheen Falls Lodge

Quark Soufflé

Quark is a fresh white cheese available in many specialty cheese stores, or you may substitute any similar fresh cheese, such as fromage frais.

2 egg whites
3 tablespoons pastry cream (recipe follows)
3 tablespoons quark cheese or fromage frais
1 tablespoon Grand Marnier, Framboise, or other liqueur (optional)
Seasonal fresh fruits such as strawberries, raspberries, or sliced
  pears or peaches, or ice cream for serving

Butter the insides of 2 individual soufflé dishes and sprinkle with granulated sugar. Refrigerate the ramekins until chilled.

Preheat the oven to 400°F (200°C). In a large bowl, beat the egg whites until stiff, glossy peaks form.

In a medium bowl, combine the pastry cream, cheese, half the beaten egg whites, and the liqueur, if using, and mix until smooth.

Carefully fold in the remaining egg whites. Spoon the mixture into the prepared ramekins until almost level with the top. Place the ramekins in a baking pan, leaving 3 to 4 inches (7.5 to 10 cm) between each soufflé, and add hot water to come halfway up the sides of the ramekins. Bake on the bottom shelf of the preheated oven for 15 to 20 minutes. Serve immediately.

Makes 2 servings

Pastry Cream
¾ cup (6 fl oz/180 ml) milk
¼ cup (2 fl oz/60 ml) heavy (whipping) cream
¼ vanilla bean, split lengthwise
2 egg yolks
½ cup (4 oz/125 g) sugar
3 tablespoons unbleached all-purpose flour
½ tablespoon cornstarch

In a medium, heavy saucepan, combine the milk, cream, and vanilla bean and bring to a boil over medium heat. In a medium bowl, beat the egg yolks and sugar together until pale in color. Add the flour and cornstarch to the egg mixture and beat or whisk until well blended. Pour in the milk mixture and mix well. Return to a clean saucepan and bring just to a boil, stirring constantly. Remove the vanilla bean and pour the mixture into a bowl. Cover with plastic wrap pressed onto the surface and let cool to room temperature.

Makes about 1½ cups (12 fl oz/375 ml)

The Shelbourne
Dublin

On the north side of St. Stephen's Green in the center of Dublin, the grand Shelbourne Hotel is an Irish institution beloved for its warmth and good humor. It has been host to royalty, nobility, actors, literary personalities, and the wealthy since 1824. James Joyce mentioned The Shelbourne in *Ulysses,* the Irish constitution was drafted in a first-floor suite in 1922, and the late Princess Grace of Monaco appreciated her private early-morning walks in the Green, away from press photographers.

The Shelbourne is just minutes away from the shops, theaters, and sights of Dublin, and the hotel's Lord Mayor's Lounge, with its piano, green silk-lined walls, high ceilings, and stunning chandelier, is the perfect Victorian setting for morning coffee or afternoon tea. It is popular with Dubliners and visitors alike as a place to meet and relax after shopping or sightseeing. The famous Horseshoe Bar has seen literary, political, and personal reputations both made and broken and is still popular with politicians and visiting celebrities.

In 1793, Lord Shelbourne's house was replaced by a townhouse, No. 27 St. Stephen's Green; today, No. 27 The Green is the name of the hotel's acclaimed restaurant. The following recipes were created by executive head chef Kevin Dundon, who combines his international experience with the very best of Irish produce, seafood, and meats to set trends and raise the standards of Irish cuisine. Chef Dundon is also in charge of the hotel's new restaurant, The Side Door, which features a more casual atmosphere and an eclectic menu.

THE MENU
The Shelbourne

The Shelbourne Chicken Salad

Scallops in Irish Whiskey and Cream Sauce

Chicken Roulades with Caramelized Apple

Chocolate Indulgence Cake

Serves Four

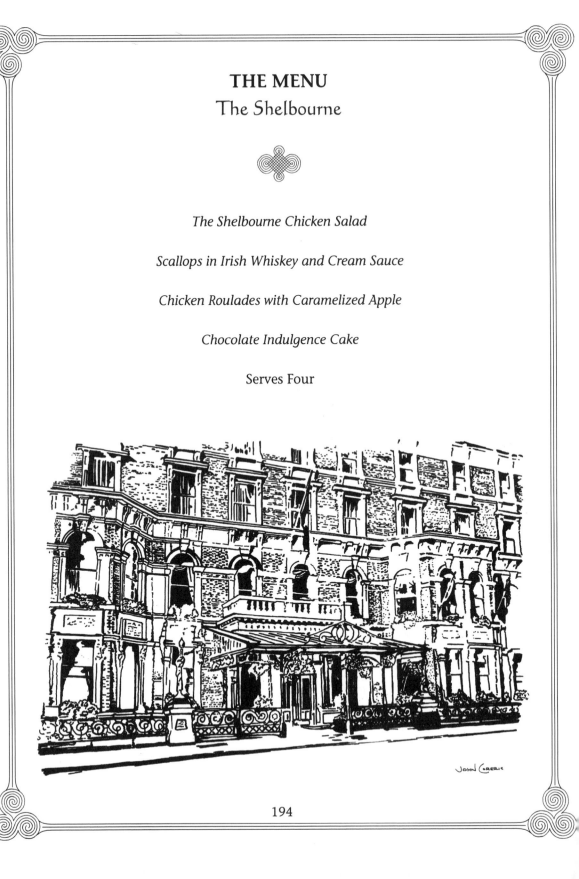

The Shelbourne Chicken Salad

This Asian-influenced salad makes a wonderful starter or a light lunch or supper dish.

Dressing
2 teaspoons minced fresh ginger
Pinch of red pepper flakes
2 tablespoons mint sauce (see page 219)
1 pinch ground nutmeg
¼ cup chopped fresh basil
Juice of 2 limes
1 cup (8 fl oz/250 ml) oyster sauce
¼ cup peanut oil

4 skinless, boneless chicken breast halves, grilled, cooled, and skinned
4 tablespoons julienned red and/or green bell peppers
2 handfuls bean sprouts
4 handfuls mixed baby greens
6 tablespoons peanuts
Deep-fried wonton strips for garnish

To make the dressing: In a blender or food processor, purée the ginger, chili, mint sauce, nutmeg, basil, lime juice, and oyster sauce. With the machine running, gradually add the oil until emulsified. Refrigerate until chilled.

Cut the chicken into julienne. In a large bowl, toss the chicken, peppers, sprouts, and greens. Toss with the dressing and serve garnished with peanuts and wonton strips.

Makes 4 servings

Scallops in Irish Whiskey and Cream Sauce

1½ tablespoons clarified butter (see page 214)
3 tablespoons minced shallots
1¼ pounds (625 g) sea scallops
1½ tablespoons Irish whiskey
¼ cup (2 fl oz/60 ml) heavy (whipping) cream
¼ cup (⅓ oz/10 g) minced fresh parsley
Salt and freshly ground black pepper to taste

In a large sauté pan or skillet, melt the butter over medium heat and sauté the shallots for 3 minutes. Add the scallops and cook for 1 minute on each side. Add the whiskey and light the pan liquid with a long match, shaking the pan until the flames subside. Stir in the cream and cook to reduce the liquid by half. Stir in the parsley, salt, and pepper. Serve immediately.

Makes 4 servings

Chicken Roulades with Caramelized Apple

4 boneless, skinless chicken breast halves
8 prunes
8 sun-dried tomatoes
½ cup (¾ oz/20 g) minced fresh parsley
Salt and freshly ground black pepper to taste
⅓ cup (3 fl oz/80 ml) Port Wine Sauce (see page 221)
2 teaspoons Sharwood curry paste
1½ tablespoons butter
⅔ cup (2¾ oz/80 g) chopped apple
1½ tablespoons packed brown sugar

Preheat the oven to 350°F (180°C). Remove the small fillet sections from the chicken breasts. In a blender or food processor, combine the chicken fillets, prunes, tomatoes, parsley, salt, and pepper; purée until smooth.

In a small saucepan, combine the port wine jus and curry paste and simmer over medium-low heat for 5 minutes.

Using the flat side of a meat pounder or the bottom of a heavy bottle, pound the chicken breast halves to a thickness of ¼ inch (6 mm). Spread the prune-tomato mixture evenly over each chicken breast and roll up from a short end. Tie with kitchen twine and place in a roasting pan. Bake in the preheated oven for 20 minutes.

In a large sauté pan or skillet, melt the butter over medium heat. Add the apple and brown sugar and cook until the apple is tender and golden brown.

Divide the caramelized apple evenly between 4 plates. Slice the chicken roulades and arrange the slices over the apples. Drizzle the sauce over the top and serve immediately.

Makes 4 servings

Chocolate Indulgence Cake

Brownie Crust

¾ cup (6 oz/185g) butter at room temperature
1¼ cup (10 oz/315 g) sugar
3 eggs
⅔ cup (3½ oz/105 g) all-purpose flour
3½ oz (105 g) bittersweet Callebaut chocolate, melted
1 cup (5 oz/155 g) ground almonds
⅓ cup (1½ oz/45 g) pecan pieces

Chocolate Mousse

6 egg yolks
¾ cup (3 oz/90 g) powdered sugar
8 ounces (250 g) bittersweet Callebaut chocolate
3 egg whites
3 tablespoons granulated sugar
2 cups (16 fl oz/500 ml) heavy (whipping) cream

To make the crust: Preheat the oven to 350°F (180°C). Butter and flour a 10-inch (25-cm) springform pan. In a large bowl, beat the butter with the sugar until pale and fluffy. Beat in the eggs one at a time until well blended. Add the flour and melted chocolate and continue beating until well blended. Stir in the ground almonds and pecan pieces.

Pour the batter into the prepared pan and bake in the preheated oven for 15 to 20 minutes, or until set. The crust should be soft but not liquid. Let cool.

To make the mousse: In a medium bowl, whisk the egg yolks and sugar together until pale. In a double boiler over barely simmering water, melt the chocolate. Remove from heat and let cool lightly. Slowly whisk the chocolate into the egg-yolk mixture.

In a small bowl, beat the egg whites and granulated sugar until stiff peaks form. In a medium bowl, beat the cream until stiff peaks form. Gently fold the egg whites and whipped cream into the chocolate mixture.

Top the brownie bottom with the mousse and refrigerate for at least 1 hour, or until ready to serve. Remove the ring, slice, and serve.

Makes one 10-inch (25-cm) cake

The Shelbourne

Tinakilly House
Rathnew, County Wicklow

A wonderful retreat for those who desire peace and quiet, Tinakilly (Irish for "house of the wood") embodies both Victorian elegance and the seafaring spirit of its first owner. The house was built in 1870 for Capt. Robert Halpin, who, as commander of the steamship *Great Eastern*, laid the first telegraph cable linking Europe and America.

Tinakilly's careful restoration has been a labor of love for proprietors Bee and William Power, who have run it as a hotel since 1983. They have augmented the Victorian-Italianate architecture with elegant antique furnishings, oil paintings, and seafaring memorabilia. The elegant country house offers twenty-six charming bedrooms, some with romantic four-poster beds, welcoming log fires, and windows with views of the Irish sea and peaceful surrounding countryside.

Guests are encouraged by the Powers and their friendly staff to "relax, eat superbly, and do nothing," or perhaps to stroll the seven acres of Victorian gardens or engage in some croquet or tennis. Golfing, horse riding, fishing, mountain drives, and historic sites are all nearby. In the dining room, chef John Moloney's acclaimed seasonal menus feature fresh fish, Wicklow lamb, game, homegrown vegetables and herbs, and a French and Irish cheese board. Bee's own delicious brown and fruit breads are baked daily, and the extensive brick wine cellar holds up to two thousand bottles.

The Menu
Tinakilly House

Roast Scallops with Mixed Peppers

Watercress Soup with Smoked Chicken

Calf's Liver with Onion Confit and Balsamic Vinegar

Vanilla Ice Cream with Warm Plums in Mulled Wine

Serves Four

JOHN GRERIS

Roast Scallops with Mixed Peppers

1 *each* red, green, and yellow bell pepper
9 tablespoons (5 fl oz/160 ml) extra-virgin olive oil
2 tablespoons minced fresh cilantro
Salt and freshly ground black pepper to taste
24 sea scallops
Juice of 1 lemon

Preheat the oven to 475°F (240°C). Put the peppers on a tray and drizzle 2 tablespoons of the olive oil over them. Roast in the preheated oven until the skin blisters and starts to burn. Remove from the oven. Cover with a piece of aluminum foil and let sit until cool enough to handle. Peel, seed, and cut the pepper into thin slices.

Pour 5 tablespoons (3 fl oz/90 ml) of the olive oil and any remaining oil in the tray that the peppers were roasted in. Add the cilantro, salt, and pepper. Warm gently to just above room temperature.

Season the scallops with lemon juice, salt, and pepper. In a large, oven-proof sauté pan or skillet over high heat, heat 2 tablespoons olive oil and sauté the scallops for 1 minute on each side, or until lightly browned. Place the pan in the oven and bake for 3 to 4 minutes.

To serve, divide the peppers and oil mixture among 4 plates, arrange 6 scallops on each plate, and serve immediately.

Makes 4 servings

Watercress Soup with Smoked Chicken

4 tablespoons (2 oz/60 g) unsalted butter
1 onion, finely chopped
2 garlic cloves, chopped
¼ cup (1 oz/30 g) chopped leek, white part only
3 large potatoes, peeled and finely diced
4 cups (32 fl oz/1 l) chicken stock (see page 213) or
    canned low-salt chicken broth
1 bunch watercress, stemmed
¾ cup (6 fl oz/180 ml) heavy (whipping) cream
Salt and freshly ground black pepper to taste
1 smoked chicken breast half, skinned, boned, and cut
    into julienne

In a large saucepan, melt the butter over medium heat. Sauté the onion, garlic, and leek for 5 minutes; do not allow them to brown. Stir in the potatoes and stock or broth and cook for 25 minutes, or until the potatoes are tender. Add the watercress and ½ cup (4 fl oz/120 ml) of the cream and cook for 1 minute. Transfer to a blender or food processor and purée. Strain the soup through a fine-meshed sieve back into the saucepan. Bring the soup just to a simmer and season with salt and pepper. Set aside and keep warm.

In a deep bowl, beat the remaining ¼ cup (2 fl oz/60 ml) cream until soft peaks form.

To serve, ladle the soup into 4 bowls. Spoon a little whipped cream on each and top with some smoked chicken.

Makes 4 servings

Calf's Liver with Onion Confit and Balsamic Vinegar

6 tablespoons (3 oz/90 g) unsalted butter
2 large onions, finely sliced
Salt and freshly ground black pepper to taste
Four 4-ounce (125-g) calf's liver slices
2 tablespoons balsamic vinegar
4 fresh chervil sprigs

To make the onion confit: In a medium, heavy sauté pan or skillet, melt 4 tablespoons (2 oz/60 g) of the butter and cook the onions over medium-low heat for 10 minutes; do not let them brown. Reduce the heat to very low and continue to cook on low heat for 1 hour, or until very tender but not browned. Transfer the onions to a blender or food processor and blend until smooth. Season with salt and pepper. Set aside and keep warm.

To prepare the liver: Season each slice with salt and pepper. In a large sauté pan or skillet, melt the remaining 2 tablespoons butter over medium heat. When the butter starts to foam, add the liver slices and sauté for 30 seconds. Turn and pour in the vinegar. Sauté for 30 seconds more. The liver will remain pink on the inside. Season with salt and pepper.

To serve, use 2 soupspoons to shape oval quenelles of onion confit and place 3 quenelles on each of 4 plates. Arrange a slice of liver in the center of each plate and drizzle the pan juices over. Garnish with the chervil and serve immediately.

Makes 4 servings

Vanilla Ice Cream with Warm Plums in Mulled Wine

Vanilla Ice Cream
2 cups (16 fl oz/500 ml) milk
2 cups (16 fl oz/500 ml) heavy (whipping) cream
2 vanilla beans, split lengthwise
10 egg yolks
½ cup (4 oz/125 g) sugar

Mulled Wine
1½ cups (12 fl oz/375 ml) dry red wine
1 cinnamon stick
Zest strips and juice of 1 orange
Zest strips and juice of 1 lemon
6 whole cloves
⅓ cup (3 oz/90 g) sugar

8 fresh plums, pitted and sliced

To make the ice cream: In a medium saucepan, combine the milk, cream, and vanilla beans and bring to a boil over medium heat, stirring constantly.

In a medium bowl, beat the egg yolks and sugar together and whisk in 1 cup of the milk mixture. Return the egg mixture to the rest of the milk, reduce heat to low, and cook, stirring constantly, until the mixture coats the back of a spoon. Remove from heat. Let cool.

Remove the vanilla beans from the mixture and freeze in an ice cream maker according to the manufacturer's instructions.

To make the mulled wine: In a medium saucepan, combine all the ingredients and bring to a low simmer over medium heat. Simmer for 5 to 10 minutes; do not let the mixture boil. Strain through a fine-meshed sieve into a bowl. Add the sliced plums.

To serve, place a scoop of ice cream in the center of each of 4 dessert plates. Arrange the plums around the ice cream and pour some mulled wine over.

Makes 4 servings

Tinakilly House

Sharon O'Connor
Irish Comfort Food from the West Coast

Currant Scones with Strawberry Preserves

Champ

Irish Stew

Sharon's Trifle

Irish Coffee

Currant Scones with Strawberry Preserves

Scones are delicious served straight from the oven with morning coffee or after-noon tea. My children enjoy them as an after-school snack.

1 cup (5 oz/155 g) whole-wheat flour
2 cups (10 oz/315 g) unbleached all-purpose flour
1 teaspoon baking soda
3 tablespoons sugar
½ teaspoon salt
⅓ cup (3 oz/90 g) cold butter, cut into pieces
⅓ cup (2 oz/60 g) dried currants
1 cup (8 fl oz/250 ml) buttermilk
1 egg, beaten
Strawberry Preserves (recipe follows)

Preheat the oven to 425°F (220°C). In a large bowl, stir the flours, baking soda, sugar, and salt until well blended. Using a pastry cutter or your fingers, cut in the butter until the mixture resembles coarse crumbs. Mix in the currants, then quickly stir in the buttermilk and egg to form a soft dough.

Turn the dough out onto a lightly floured work surface and pat it to a ¾-inch (2-cm) thickness. Using a 2-inch-diameter (5-cm) glass or cookie cutter, cut the dough into rounds and place on a baking sheet. Bake in the preheated oven for 15 to 20 minutes, or until golden brown.

Makes about 16 scones

Sharon O'Connor

Strawberry Preserves

When strawberries are in season, easy-to-make preserves are a great way to cap-ture their flavor. This recipe may be doubled.

1 basket fresh strawberries, hulled
¾ cup (6 oz/185 g) sugar

Place the strawberries in a medium, heavy saucepan and mash them coarsely. Cook the strawberries over medium heat, stirring frequently, until they begin to thicken, about 10 minutes. Reduce heat to low, add the sugar, and stir until it dissolves. Increase heat to medium and boil, stirring frequently, for 20 minutes, or until the mixture thickens enough to mound on a spoon. Remove from heat and let cool. Store in a covered container in the refrigerator for up to 1 week.

Makes about 1½ cups (15 oz/470 g)

Sharon O'Connor

Champ

This traditional Irish dish of mashed potatoes with green onions is delicious served with grilled sausages, steak, or chops. Serve piping hot and make a crater in the center of each serving to hold a lump of butter; each mouthful is dipped into the melted butter.

2 pounds (1 kg) unpeeled baking potatoes, scrubbed
1 cup (8 fl oz/250 ml) milk
4 tablespoons (2 oz/60 g) butter
6 green onions, including some green tops, finely chopped
Salt and freshly ground black pepper to taste

Cook the potatoes in a large pot of salted boiling water until tender, about 20 minutes. Meanwhile, in a small saucepan, melt the butter over low heat and add the milk and green onions; simmer while the potatoes are cooking. Drain, peel, and mash the potatoes. Beat in the milk mixture until smooth. Serve immediately.

Makes 4 servings

Sharon O'Connor

Irish Stew

Simply prepared, substantial, and satisfying, this dish is one of the oldest Irish recipes in existence. It is especially delicious accompanied with fresh brown bread and a glass of Guinness. Although the classic version doesn't include carrots, I like to use them.

3 pounds (1.4 kg) boneless lamb from the neck or shoulder,
    trimmed and cut into 1½-inch (4-cm) pieces
3 potatoes, peeled and cut into ¼-inch (6-mm) slices
3 onions, sliced
3 carrots, peeled and quartered
Salt and freshly ground black pepper to taste
2 tablespoons minced fresh parsley
2 cups (16 fl oz/500 ml) water, lamb stock, or beef broth

Sprinkle the lamb with salt and pepper. In a large, heavy pot or Dutch oven, layer half of the potatoes, and all the lamb, onions, and carrots, sprinkling each layer with salt, pepper, and parsley. Top with a layer of the remaining potatoes. Pour the water, lamb stock, or beef broth over. Cover the pot with aluminum foil and then a lid. Place the pot over high heat and bring to a boil, then reduce heat to low and simmer for about 2 hours or until tender. Alternatively, the stew may be baked in a preheated 325°F (165°C) oven for 2 hours once it has come to a boil.

Makes 4 to 6 servings

Sharon O'Connor

Sharon's Trifle

Serve this perfect party dessert in your most beautiful glass bowl. The cake may be made up to 2 days before serving.

Custard Sauce

2 cups (16 fl oz/500 ml) milk

5 egg yolks

⅓ cup (3 oz/90 g) granulated sugar

1 teaspoon vanilla extract

Sponge Cake

6 eggs

1 cup (8 oz/250 g) granulated sugar

1 cup (5 oz/155 g) unbleached all-purpose flour

½ cup (4 oz/125 g) butter, melted

2 teaspoons vanilla extract

1 basket fresh raspberries

4 tablespoons powdered sugar, sifted

2 cups (16 fl oz/500 ml) heavy (whipping) cream

1 teaspoon vanilla extract

¾ cup (6 fl oz/180 ml) dry sherry

2 cups (8 oz/250 g) mixed fresh fruit such as blueberries, sliced
    strawberries, peaches, and pears

Fresh raspberries or strawberries for garnish

To make the custard sauce: In a heavy, medium saucepan, heat the milk over medium heat until bubbles form around the edges of the pan. In a small bowl, whisk together the egg yolks and sugar until the mixture is thick and pale in color. Gradually whisk the hot milk into the egg mixture. Return the mixture to the saucepan and cook over low heat, stirring constantly, until the mixture thickens enough to coat a spoon.

Remove from heat and pour into a clean bowl. Stir in the vanilla and let cool completely. To make ahead, cover and refrigerate for up to 24 hours.

To make the sponge cake: Preheat the oven to 350°F (180°C). Butter and flour two 10-inch (25-cm) round cake pans. In a large bowl, beat the eggs and sugar together until thick and pale in color; the volume should increase threefold. Sift half of the flour over and fold it in. Dribble the butter over the batter and fold it in. Sift the remaining flour over and fold it in, along with the vanilla extract.

Divide the batter between the prepared pans and bake in the preheated oven for 20 minutes, or until a toothpick inserted in the center of each cake comes out clean. Let cool for 10 minutes. Remove the cakes from the pans and let cool completely on wire racks.

Purée the raspberries and 1 tablespoon of the powdered sugar in a blender or food processor until smooth. In a deep bowl, whip 1 cup (8 fl oz/250 ml) of the cream until stiff peaks form. Fold in 1 tablespoon of the powdered sugar and ½ teaspoon of the vanilla.

Place 1 cake layer in the bottom of a large glass bowl and pour the sherry over. Spread the cake with half the raspberry purée and spread half the custard sauce over the purée. Add half the fruit and the whipped cream. Repeat with the remaining cake, purée, and fruit. Pour the custard sauce over all. Loosely cover the bowl with plastic wrap and refrigerate for at least 3 hours.

Just before serving, whip the remaining 1 cup (8 fl oz/250 ml) cream in a deep bowl until soft peaks form. Fold in the remaining 2 tablespoons of powdered sugar and ½ teaspoon vanilla. Dollop the whipped cream over the trifle, garnish with fresh raspberries or strawberries, and serve immediately.

Makes 8 to 10 servings

Sharon O'Connor

Irish Coffee

Although this is not a traditional Irish drink, it's well on the way to becoming one. Irish coffee is served in most pubs and restaurants in Ireland and is a delightful finish for a meal.

½ cup (4 fl oz/125 ml) heavy (whipping) cream
6 teaspoons sugar
3 cups (24 fl oz/750 ml) hot strong coffee
12 tablespoons (6 fl oz/180 ml) Irish whiskey

In a deep bowl, beat the cream until soft peaks form. Beat in 4 teaspoons of the sugar. Cover and refrigerate up to 30 minutes.

Warm 4 stemmed glasses by running very hot water into them; dry. Add ½ teaspoon of the sugar to each glass, then pour hot coffee into each glass to fill to within 1½ inches of the top; stir to dissolve the sugar. Add 3 tablespoons Irish whiskey to each glass. Spoon a quarter of the whipped cream over each serving and serve at once.

Makes 4 servings

Sharon O'Connor

BASICS

Butter Sauce

1¼ cups (10 oz/300 ml) dry white wine

1 teaspoon fresh lemon juice

½ cup (4 oz/125 g) butter, cut into pieces

In a small saucepan, heat the wine and lemon juice over high heat and cook to reduce by one-third. Add the butter and whisk until it melts. Serve immediately.

Makes about ½ cup (4 fl oz/125 ml)

Mustard Seed Butter Sauce

Whisk 1 tablespoon whole-grain mustard, or to taste, into the above butter sauce after the butter has melted. Serve warm.

Chicken Stock

About 4 pounds (2 kg) bony chicken pieces (backs and necks)

1 onion, chopped

1 carrot, peeled and chopped

3 celery stalks, chopped

8 fresh parsley sprigs

Salt and freshly ground pepper to taste (optional)

Put the chicken pieces in a large stockpot. Add water to cover by 1 inch (2.5 cm). Bring to a slow boil, occasionally skimming off any foam that rises to the surface. Add the vegetables. Cover the pan, reduce heat to a simmer, and cook for 1 hour, adding water as necessary to keep the ingredients covered. Strain through a sieve into a large bowl. Add salt and pepper if you like. Refrigerate for several hours, or until the fat has congealed. Remove and discard the congealed fat. Store in the refrigerator for up to 3 days. To keep longer, bring to a boil every 3 days, or freeze for up to 3 months.

Makes about 8 cups (64 fl oz/2 l)

Clarified Butter

In a heavy saucepan, melt unsalted butter over low heat. Remove the pan from heat and let stand for several minutes. Skim off the foam and pour off the clear liquid, leaving the milky solids in the bottom of the pan. Cover and store in the refrigerator indefinitely. When clarified, butter loses about one-fourth its original volume.

Cumberland Sauce
An excellent tangy-sweet sauce to serve with ham, venison, or duck.

1 orange
1 lemon
1 cup red currant jelly
½ cup port or red wine
1 teaspoon arrowroot
1 tablespoon water

Using a vegetable peeler, remove the zest from the orange and lemon and cut into fine shreds. In a small saucepan of boiling water, blanch the zest for 3 minutes, then drain and rinse with cold water; set aside.

Squeeze the juice from the orange and lemon. In a small saucepan, combine the juices and jelly, and bring to a boil. Reduce heat to a simmer and stir in the port or wine. Simmer for 5 minutes; remove from heat. Mix the arrowroot with the water to make a paste and add to the juice mixture. Return to high heat and cook, stirring constantly, for 1 minute, or until the sauce thickens and clears. Remove from heat and stir in the blanched zest. Cover and refrigerate for at least 24 hours before using.

Makes about 2 cups (16 fl oz/500 ml)

Custard Sauce

3 eggs, lightly beaten
¼ cup sugar
¼ teaspoon salt
2 cups (16 fl oz/500 ml) milk, scalded
½ to 1 teaspoon vanilla extract

In a heavy, medium saucepan over medium heat, whisk the eggs, sugar, salt, and milk together. Stir constantly until the mixture thickens enough to coat the back of a spoon. Remove from heat and place the pan in a bowl of cold water, stirring for a minute or two. Stir in the vanilla, cover with plastic wrap placed directly on top of the sauce, and refrigerate for up to 24 hours.

Makes about 2½ cups (20 fl oz/625 ml)

Whiskey-Flavored Custard Sauce

Add ¼ cup whiskey to the milk along with the other ingredients in the above recipe.

Digestive Biscuits

These are really a cross between cookies and crackers. Serve them for tea, or grind them to use in a crumb pie crust.

¼ cup (45 g) all-purpose flour
1¼ cups (200 g) whole-wheat flour
⅓ cup (30 g) oatmeal
1 tablespoon sugar
½ teaspoon baking soda
1 teaspoon baking powder
½ teaspoon salt
6 tablespoons (90 g) cold butter
Milk, as needed

Preheat the oven to 350°F (180°C). In a medium bowl, combine the

215

flours, oats, sugar, salt, baking soda, and baking powder and stir to mix thoroughly. Using a pastry cutter or 2 knives, cut in the butter until the mixture is the texture of coarse meal. Stir in the milk to make a soft dough. On a floured surface, lightly knead the dough until smooth, about 1 minute. Roll the dough out and cut into biscuits with a 2-inch (5-cm) round cutter. Place the biscuits 1 inch (2.5 cm) apart on a greased baking sheet and prick each biscuit with a fork. Bake in the preheated oven for 12 to 15 minutes, or until lightly browned. Transfer to a wire rack to cool completely. Store in an airtight container.

Makes about 20 biscuits

Duck Stock
3 pounds (1.5 kg) duck bones and trimmings
1 cup (8 fl oz/250 ml) dry red wine
1 onion, chopped
1 large carrot, peeled and chopped
1 celery stalk, chopped
1 leek, including some of the green leaves, cleaned and chopped
9 fresh parsley sprigs
Salt and freshly ground black pepper to taste (optional)

Preheat the oven to 450°F (230°C). Rinse the bones and trimmings. Put the bones and trimmings in a roasting pan and bake in the preheated oven, turning once or twice, for 30 minutes, or until deep brown. Transfer to a stockpot and drain the fat from the roasting pan.

Place the roasting pan over medium heat and add the wine to the pan. Stir to scrape up the browned bits on the bottom of the pan. Add this liquid to the stockpot along with the onion, carrot, celery, leek, and parsley. Add water to cover by 1 inch (2.5 cm) and bring to a boil over high heat. Skim the surface to remove any foam that rises to the top. Reduce heat to a simmer and cook uncovered for 3 to 4 hours, adding water as needed to keep the ingredients covered. Add salt and pepper if you like. Strain through a sieve.

Cover and refrigerate for several hours, or until the fat congeals on the surface. Remove and discard the congealed fat. Store in the refrigerator for up to 3 days. To keep longer, bring to a boil every 3 days, or freeze for up to 3 months.

Makes about 6 cups (48 fl oz/1.5 l)

Fish Stock
1½ pounds (750 g) fish heads, bones, and trimmings
1 celery stalk, chopped
1 onion, chopped
1 carrot, peeled and chopped
1 bay leaf
4 fresh parsley sprigs
½ cup (4 fl oz/125 ml) dry white wine
Salt and freshly ground black pepper to taste (optional)

Rinse the fish parts. In a stockpot, put the fish parts, celery, onion, carrot, bay leaf, parsley, wine, and water to cover by 1 inch (2.5 cm). Bring to a boil and skim off the foam as it rises to the surface. Cover and simmer for 20 minutes. Remove from heat, let cool to room temperature, and strain through a sieve. Add salt and pepper if you like.

Cover and store in the refrigerator for up to 3 days. To keep longer, bring to a boil every 3 days or freeze for up to 3 months.

Makes about 6 cups (48 fl oz/1.5 l)

Lamb Stock
Uncooked bones and trimmings from 1 leg of lamb
1 carrot, peeled and chopped
1 onion, chopped
1 cup (8 fl oz/250 ml) water
1 celery stalk, chopped
2 garlic cloves, crushed

1 bay leaf

¼ teaspoon minced fresh rosemary

Salt and freshly ground black pepper to taste (optional)

Preheat the oven to 425°F (220°C). Put the bones and trimmings, carrot, and onion in a roasting pan and bake in the preheated oven, turning occasionally, for 30 to 40 minutes, or until browned. Transfer the bones and vegetables to a stockpot and drain the fat from the roasting pan.

Place the roasting pan over medium heat and add the water. Stir to scrape up the browned bits from the bottom of the pan. Pour the pan liquid into the pot with the bones. Add water to cover the ingredients by 1 inch (2.5 cm) and bring to a simmer. Skim off any foam that rises to the surface. Add the chopped celery, garlic, bay leaf, and rosemary. Cover and simmer for 3 to 4 hours, adding water as needed to keep the ingredients covered.

Strain through a sieve into a bowl and add salt and pepper, if you like. Refrigerate for several hours until the fat congeals. Remove and discard the congealed fat. Cover and store in the refrigerator for up to 3 days. To keep longer, bring to a boil every 3 days.

Makes about 8 cups (64 fl oz/2 l)

Lobster Stock

Shell from 1 cooked lobster

1 onion, thinly sliced

1 carrot, peeled and sliced

1 celery stalk, sliced

10 white peppercorns

2 fresh thyme sprigs

2 bay leaves

10 cups (2¼ qt/2.5 l) cold water

1 tablespoon tomato paste
Salt and freshly ground white pepper to taste (optional)

In a stockpot, combine all the ingredients except the salt and pepper. Bring to a slow boil and cook to reduce to 3 cups (24 fl oz/750 ml). Strain the stock through a sieve and add salt and pepper if you like. Cover and store in the refrigerator for up to 3 days. To keep longer, bring to a boil every 3 days or freeze for up to 3 months.

Makes 3 cups (24 fl oz/750 ml)

Mint Sauce
This is the traditional Irish accompaniment for lamb.

2 tablespoons minced fresh mint leaves
2 tablespoons boiling water
2 tablespoons sugar
2 tablespoons white wine vinegar

In a small bowl, combine the mint and sugar, add the water and stir until the sugar is dissolved, then stir in the vinegar. Let sit for at least 30 minutes before using.

Makes about ½ cup (4 fl oz/125 ml)

Pastry Dough
The choice of salt or sugar will depend on whether the filling is savory or sweet.

1 ¾ cups (9 oz/280 g) all-purpose flour
Pinch of salt or 2 teaspoons sugar
½ cup (4 oz/125 g) cold butter, lard, shortening, or a combination,
  cut into small pieces
3 to 4 tablespoons cold water

In a medium bowl, stir the flour and salt or sugar together. Cut the fat into the flour mixture with a pastry cutter or 2 knives until the pieces are well coated with flour. Rub the fat into the flour with your fingertips until the mixture resembles fine bread crumbs.

Add 2 to 3 tablespoons of the water and mix quickly with a fork. Press the dough together with your fingers, adding the remaining 1 tablespoon water, if necessary, to make a firm dough.

On a floured work surface, lightly knead the dough for a few seconds until smooth. Form into a disk, wrap in plastic, and refrigerate for at least 30 minutes before rolling out.

Makes enough pastry for an 8- or 9-inch (20- or 23-cm) single-crust pie

Peeling and Seeding Tomatoes

Cut out the cores of the tomatoes and cut an X in the opposite end. Drop the tomatoes into a pot of rapidly boiling water for 10 seconds, or until the skin by the X peels away slightly. Drain and run cold water over the tomatoes; the skin should slip off easily. To seed, cut the tomatoes in half crosswise, hold each half upside down over the sink, and gently squeeze and shake to remove the seeds.

Pesto

6 tablespoons (3 fl oz/90 ml) olive oil
1 cup fresh basil leaves
1 tablespoon pine nuts
1 garlic clove, chopped
½ teaspoon salt
⅓ cup (1½ oz/45 g) grated Parmesan and/or pecorino romano cheese

Put the olive oil, then the basil, pine nuts, garlic, and salt in a blender or food processor and blend, occasionally scraping the sides with a spatula. Transfer to a bowl and stir in the cheese.

Makes about 1 cup (8 fl oz/250 ml)

Pheasant Stock

Pheasant giblets (heart, gizzard, neck, and liver)
2 tablespoons butter
1 small onion, quartered
1 small carrot, peeled and sliced
2½ cups (20 fl oz/625 ml) water
1 bay leaf
6 peppercorns
Salt to taste (optional)

Rinse and dry the giblets. In a medium saucepan, melt the butter over medium heat and sauté the giblets, onion, and carrot until they begin to brown, about 10 minutes. Add the water, bay leaf, and peppercorns. Bring to a boil, then reduce heat and simmer for 1 hour. Strain through a sieve and add salt, if you like.

Refrigerate for several hours until the fat congeals. Remove and discard the fat. Store in the refrigerator for up to 3 days. To keep longer, bring to a boil every 3 days or freeze for up to 3 months.

Makes about 2 cups (16 fl oz/500 ml)

Port Wine Sauce
This sauce is excellent with venison and duck.

2 tablespoons plus 1 teaspoon butter
1 tablespoon minced shallot
¼ cup (2 fl oz/60 ml) port wine
1 cup (8 fl oz/250 ml) chicken stock (see page 213)
   or canned low-salt chicken broth
1 teaspoon minced fresh parsley
Salt and freshly ground black pepper to taste
1 teaspoon all-purpose flour

In a small saucepan, melt the 2 tablespoons butter over medium heat and sauté the shallot for 2 minutes; do not let it brown. Add the port, raise heat to high, and bring to a boil until the liquid is reduced by half. Add the stock or broth, parsley, salt, and pepper.

In a small sauté pan over low heat, melt the 1 teaspoon butter, stir in the flour, and cook for 1 minute, stirring constantly. Whisk in the port mixture. Cook, stirring constantly, for 3 minutes, or until slightly thickened. Serve warm.

Makes about 1½ cups (12 fl oz/375ml)

Potato Chips
2 baking potatoes, peeled
2 cups (16 fl oz/500 ml) corn oil

Cut the potatoes into ⅛ inch-thick (2-mm) slices, putting them in cold water to cover as you slice them.

Drain the potatoes and pat them dry on paper towels. In a heavy pot or deep fryer over medium-high heat, heat the oil until almost smoking. Add the potato slices in small batches and cook until golden brown. Using a slotted spoon, remove the chips and drain on paper towels. Serve immediately.

Red Wine Sauce
2 pounds (1 kg) beef bones
2 tablespoons olive oil
1 onion, chopped
1 carrot, peeled and chopped
1 celery stalk, chopped
1 small leek, chopped
1 tablespoon minced fresh parsley
1 teaspoon minced fresh rosemary
1 teaspoon minced fresh thyme
5 whole peppercorns
2 cups (16 fl oz/500 ml) dry red wine

2 cups (16 fl oz/500 ml) beef stock or canned beef broth
1 cup (8 fl oz/250 ml) water
Salt and freshly ground black pepper to taste

Preheat the oven to 450°F (230°C). Put the bones in a roasting pan and bake in the preheated oven for 30 minutes, or until well browned. Remove the bones from the roasting pan and set them aside. Pour off the fat from the pan.

Place the roasting pan over medium heat, add the olive oil, and sauté the onion for 5 minutes, or until translucent. Add the carrot, celery, leek parsley, rosemary, thyme, and peppercorns and sauté until the vegetables are slightly browned. Pour in ½ cup (4 fl oz/125 ml) of the red wine and stir to scrape up the browned bits from the bottom of the pan. Raise the heat to high and cook to reduce to a glaze. Add the bones, the remaining 1½ cups (12 fl oz/375 ml) wine, the stock or broth, and water and bring to a boil. Skim off any fat, reduce heat to low, and simmer for 1 hour. Strain through a fine-meshed sieve. Refrigerate for several hours until the fat has congealed. Discard the fat and return to high heat. Cook to reduce by half. Add salt and pepper.

Makes about 2½ cups (20 fl oz/625 ml)

Reduced Stock or Broth

Use unsalted or low-salt stock or broth. Cook over medium heat at a low boil until reduced by about one-third, or until rich and well flavored.

Roasting Peppers

Char peppers over a gas flame or under a preheated broiler until the skin is blackened all over. Using tongs, transfer the peppers to a paper or plastic bag, close it, and let the peppers cool for 10 to 15 minutes. Remove from the bag, peel off the skin with your fingers or a small, sharp knife, and core and seed the peppers.

Simple Syrup

In a small, heavy saucepan, combine 1 cup (8 oz/250 g) sugar and ½ cup (4 fl oz/125 ml) water and bring to a simmer over medium heat. When the sugar has dissolved, remove from heat and let cool. Place in an airtight container and store in the refrigerator for 6 months or longer.

Toasting Nuts

Preheat the oven to 350°F (180°C). Spread the nuts on a baking sheet and bake for 5 to 10 minutes, or until fragrant and very lightly browned, stirring once or twice. Store in an airtight container in the refrigerator or freezer.

Toasting and Peeling Hazelnuts

Preheat the oven to 350°F (180°C). Spread the nuts on a baking sheet and bake for 10 to 15 minutes or until lightly browned, stirring once or twice. Remove from the oven, fold in a kitchen towel, and let cool for 5 minutes. Rub the hazelnuts with the towel to remove the skins. Pour the nuts into a colander and shake it over the sink to discard the remaining skins.

Vanilla Sugar

Place 3 cups (1½ lb/750 g) granulated sugar in a glass jar. Split a vanilla bean in half, scrape the seeds from each half, and cut the two halves into ½-inch (12-mm) pieces. Add the pieces and the seeds to the sugar, tightly close the jar, and store for at least 1 week, shaking occasionally. Pour the sugar through a sieve as you use it, returning the beans and seeds to the jar. Refill the jar with fresh sugar, as needed. (This may be repeated for up to 6 months, or until the vanilla flavor weakens.)

Makes about 3 cups (1½ lb/750 g)

Veal Stock

2 pounds (1 kg) veal bones
2 tablespoons vegetable oil
1 onion, chopped
1 carrot, peeled and chopped
1 celery stalk, chopped
½ cup (4 fl oz/125 ml) dry white wine
Salt and freshly ground white pepper to taste (optional)

Preheat the oven to 400°F (200°C). In a roasting pan, toss the bones with the oil and vegetables. Bake in the preheated oven until browned, 30 to 40 minutes, turning occasionally. Transfer the bones and vegetables to a large stockpot.

Pour the fat out of the roasting pan. Place the pan over medium heat and add the wine, stirring to scrape up the browned bits on the bottom of the pan. Pour the pan liquid into the saucepan with the bones and vegetables. Add water to cover the ingredients by 1 inch (2.5 cm). Bring to a boil and skim off any foam that rises to the top. Cover and simmer for 3 to 4 hours.

Strain through a sieve into a bowl and add salt and pepper if you like. Refrigerate for several hours until the fat has congealed. Remove and discard the congealed fat. Store in the refrigerator for up to 3 days. For longer storage, bring to a boil every 3 days or freeze for up to 3 months.

Makes about 4 cups (32 fl oz/1 l)

Vegetable Stock

2 carrots, peeled and chopped
5 onions, chopped
1 fennel bulb, trimmed and chopped
2 leeks, white part only, cleaned and chopped
1 celery stalk, chopped
9 garlic cloves, crushed
8 peppercorns

3 oz/90 g chopped fresh herbs, or 1 oz/30 g dried herbs
Salt to taste (optional)

In a stockpot, combine all the vegetables. Add cold water to cover and bring to a boil. Skim off any foam that rises to the surface and simmer for 30 minutes. Add the peppercorns and herbs and simmer for 1 minute. Remove from heat and strain through a fine-meshed sieve. Add salt, if you like, and let cool.

Cover and refrigerate for up to 3 days. To keep longer, bring to a boil every 3 days or freeze for up to 3 months.

Makes about 3 quarts (3 l)

CONVERSION CHARTS

Weight Measurements

Standard U.S.	Ounce	Metric
1 ounce	1	30 g
¼ pound	4	125 g
½ pound	8	250 g
1 pound	16	500 g
1½ pounds	24	750 g
2 pounds	32	1 kg
2½ pounds	40	1.25 kg
3 pounds	48	1.5 kg

Volume Measurements

Standard U.S.	Fluid Ounces	Metric
1 tablespoon	½	15 ml
2 tablespoons	1	30 ml
3 tablespoons	1½	45 ml
¼ cup (4 T)	2	60 ml
6 tablespoons	3	90 ml
½ cup (8 T)	4	125 ml
1 cup	8	250 ml
1 pint (2 cups)	16	500 ml
4 cups	32	1 l

Oven Temperatures

Fahrenheit	Celsius	Gas Mark
250°	120°	½
275°	135°	1
300°	150°	2
325°	165°	3
350°	180°	4
375°	190°	5
400°	200°	6
425°	220°	7

Note: For ease of use, measurements have been rounded off.

Conversion Factors

Ounces to grams: Multiply the ounce figure by 28.3 to get the number of grams.

Pounds to grams: Multiply the pound figure by 453.59 to get the number of grams.

Pounds to kilograms: Multiply the pound figure by 0.45 to get the number of kilograms.

Ounces to milliliters: Multiply the ounce figure by 30 to get the number of milliliters.

Cups to liters: Multiply the cup figure by 0.24 to get the number of liters.

Fahrenheit to Celsius: Subtract 32 from the Fahrenheit figure, multiply by 5, then divide by 9 to get the Celsius figure.

LIST OF CONTRIBUTORS

Adare Manor
Adare, County
Limerick, Ireland
Tel. 353-061-396566 /
U.S. 800-462-3273
Fax 353-061-396124 /
201-467-1965

Ashford Castle
Cong, County Mayo,
Ireland
Tel. 353-092-46003
Fax 353-092-46260

**Assolas Country
House**
Kanturk, County Cork,
Ireland
Tel. 353-029-50015
Fax 353-029-50795

**Ballylickey Manor
House**
Ballylickey, Bantry Bay,
County Cork, Ireland
Tel. 353-027-50071
Fax 353-027-50124

Caragh Lodge
Caragh Lake, County
Kerry, Ireland
Tel. 353-066-69115
Fax 353-066-69316

Cashel House
Cashel, County
Galway, Ireland
Tel. 353-095-31001
Fax 353-095-31077

Coopershill House
Riverstown, County
Sligo, Ireland
Tel. 353-071-65108
Fax 353-071-65466

Drimcong House
Moycullen, County
Galway, Ireland
Tel. 353-091-85115

Dromoland Castle
Newmarket-on-Fergus,
County Clare, Ireland
Tel. 353-061-368144
Fax 353-061-363355

Gregans Castle
Ballyvaughan, County
Clare, Ireland
Tel. 353-065-77005
Fax 353-065-77111

Hunter's Hotel
Rathnew
County Wicklow,
Ireland
Tel. 353-404-40106
Fax 353-404-40338

**Kildare Hotel &
Country Club**
At Straffan, County
Kildare, Ireland
Tel. 353-1-627-3333
Fax 353-1-627-3312

Longueville House
Mallow, County Cork,
Ireland
Tel. 353-022-47156
Fax 353-022-47459

Marlfield House
Gorey, County
Wexford, Ireland
Tel. 353-055-21124
Fax 353-055-21572

Newport House
Newport, County Mayo,
Ireland
Tel. 353-098-41222
Fax 353-098-41613

The Old Rectory
Wicklow, County
Wicklow, Ireland
Tel. 353-404-67048
Fax 353-404-69181

Park Hotel Kenmare
Kenmare, County
Kerry, Ireland
Tel. 353-064-41200
Fax 353-064-41402

Rathmullan House
Rathmullan,
Letterkenny, County
Donegal, Ireland
Tel. 353-074-58188
Fax 353-074-58200

Rathsallagh House
Dunlavin, County
Wicklow, Ireland
Tel. 353-045-53112
Fax 353-045-53343

**Rosleague Manor
Hotel**
Letterfrack, County
Galway, Ireland
Tel. 353-095-41101
Fax 353-095-41168

Sheen Falls Lodge
Kenmare, County
Kerry, Ireland
Tel. 353-64-41600
Fax 353-64-41386

The Shelbourne
27 St. Stephen's Green
Dublin 2, Ireland
Tel. 353-1-676-6471
Fax 353-1-661-6006

Tinakilly House
Rathnew, County
Wicklow, Ireland
Tel. 353-404-69274
Fax 353-404-67806

ACKNOWLEDGMENTS

I would like to thank the many people who made this volume possible.

My deepest gratitude to the proprietors and chefs who generously contributed menus and recipes to the cookbook: Gerard Castelloe; Stephen Quinn; Denis Lenihan; Rory Murphy; Hazel and Joe Bourke; Christiane and George Graves; Mary Gaunt; Kay and Dermot McEvilly; Lindy and Brian O'Hara; Gerry and Marie Galvin; Mark Nolan; Jean-Baptiste Molinari; Peter, Moira, and Simon Haden; the Gelletlie family; John Sutton; Michel Flamme; Michael, Jane, and William O'Callaghan; Mary and Ray Bowe; Kieran and Thelma Thompson; Linda and Paul Saunders; Francis Brennan; Bob and Robin Wheeler; Kay and Joe O'Flynn; Anne and Patrick Foyle; Nigel Rush; Fergus Moore; Kevin Dundon; Donal O'Gallagher; William and Bee Power; and John Moloney. Thanks also to chef Guillaume Lequin at Rathsallagh House.

Special thanks to Don Meade, for his wonderful notes on the music. Thanks also are due to Robin Adams and Stuart O Seanóir at Trinity College Library, and to Orla Carey and Mary Orla Duke of the Irish Tourist Board in New York. Thank you, Sybil Connolly, for the beautiful fabric.

Once again, I am so glad to have Carolyn Miller to thank for her thoughtful editing. Grateful acknowledgments are due to Sharilyn Hovind, Eric Liebau, Ned Waring, Tim Forney, Jim Armstrong, Steve Patterson, and to the rest of the staff at Menus and Music. Michael Osborne and Tom Kamegai deserve many thanks for their wonderful design and support of this project. Thank you, John Coreris, for the splendid architectural illustrations.

I am forever grateful to James Keane for making this recording a dream come true. Affectionate and grateful thanks to flutist Seamus Egan, violinist Winnie Horan, and celtic harpist Sue Richards. Thanks to recording and mixing engineer Greg Anderson for his dedication, to mixing engineer Gary Clayton, and once again to George Horn for the digital mastering. Thank you, Patrick Clancy and Henry Counihan.

Thanks, Dad, for the foreword and for passing on your love of music, words, and fine food and as always, to my Irish roving girls, Claire and Caitlin, and to my husband, John, for their love.

INDEX

Eliot Khuner

Sharon O'Connor is a musician, author, and cook. The founder of the San Francisco String Quartet, she is also the creator of the Menus and Music series, which combines her love of music and food. She lives in the San Francisco Bay Area with her husband and two daughters. *The Irish Isle* is the eleventh volume in her series of cookbooks with musical recordings.